Optimize Your Cruising Sailboat

Optimize Your Cruising Sailboat

101 WAYS TO MAKE YOUR SAILBOAT BETTER

John Roberts

Camden, Maine · New York · San Francisco · Washington, D.C. · Auckland
Bogotá · Caracas · Lisbon · London · Madrid · Mexico City · Milan
Montreal · New Delhi · San Juan · Singapore · Sydney · Tokyo ·Toronto

Also by John Roberts

The Boating Book: A Practical Guide to Safe Pleasure Boating, Power and Sail

Choosing Your Boat: A Practical Guide to Selecting a Sailboat That Fits Your Pocketbook and Your Sailing Needs (with Maria Mann)

Fiberglass Boats: Construction, Repair, and Maintenance

Why Didn't I Think of That? (with Susan Roberts)

The **McGraw·Hill** Companies

3 4 5 6 7 8 9 0 DOC DOC 0 9 8 7 6

ISBN: 978-0-07-141951-2
MHID: 0-07-141951-9

The Library of Congress has cataloged the cloth edition as follows:
Roberts, John, 1938–
   Optimize your cruising sailboat : 101 ways to make your sailboat better /
     John Roberts
        p.   cm.
   Includes bibliographical references and index.
   ISBN 0-07-134114-5 (alk. paper)
   1. Sailboats. 2. Sailboats—Maintenance and repair. I. Title.
VM351 .R6324 2000
623.8′223—dc21   00-022835

Paperback ISBN 0-07-141951-9

Questions regarding the content of this book should be addressed to
International Marine
P.O. Box 220
Camden, ME 04843
www.internationalmarine.com

Questions regarding the ordering of this book should be addressed to
The McGraw-Hill Companies
Customer Service Department
P.O. Box 547
Blacklick, OH 43004
Retail customers: 1-800-262-4729
Bookstores: 1-800-722-4726

Printed by R.R. Donnelley, Crawfordsville, IN; Design by Books by Design; Illustrations by Jim Sollers; Photographs by the author; Production management by Janet Robbins; Page layout by Shannon Thomas; Edited by Jon Eaton and Joanne Allen

The author has made all effort to reproduce trademarked terms accurately.

Contents

Acknowledgments

*M*any people contributed importantly to this book by making themselves available to answer my questions, often offering ideas that have ended up somewhere in these pages. These people include Brad Mack at Mack Sails, Tom Wohlgemuth at Chesapeake Rigging and Annapolis Spars, Ted Brewer of Brewer Yacht Designs, Don Pussehl at Fawcett Boat Supplies, representatives of too many marine systems and equipment manufacturers to list individually, yacht brokers, and the owners of hundreds of boats at shows of new and used boats, docks, and in the work areas of boatyards. Many of these boats provided grist for this book. Finally, I must thank my friend, sailing partner, and wife, Susan. She has read every word in these pages too many times, asking questions and offering comments that have made us all the beneficiaries of her time and effort.

Introduction

*T*his book is for sailors who enjoy cruising on their boats. I use the word *cruising* in its broadest sense, to mean anything from weekending to circling the globe. And by *boats* I mean sailboats ranging from about 24 to about 45 feet.

Optimize Your Cruising Sailboat is based on the notion that sailors generally are on the lookout for ways to upgrade their boats. In fact, I gathered many of the ideas included here by looking at hundreds of boats and talking to lots of people about what might be done to make those boats more comfortable, easier to handle, more seaworthy, faster, and better looking.

The suggestions offered in these pages range from relatively modest improvements that can be easily undertaken by most sailors to some fairly major changes that should be carried out by professionals. Many of these suggestions, of course, involve some kind of hardware or equipment. For the most part, these items are available worldwide from one of three sources: major marine chandleries, directly from their manufacturers, or through the manufacturers' international subsidiaries (see appendix). Alternatively, competitive items of local manufacture may be available. Finally, although I've used the standard English system of weights and measures in the text, a metric conversion table is included after the appendix for the convenience of sailors more accustomed to the metric system.

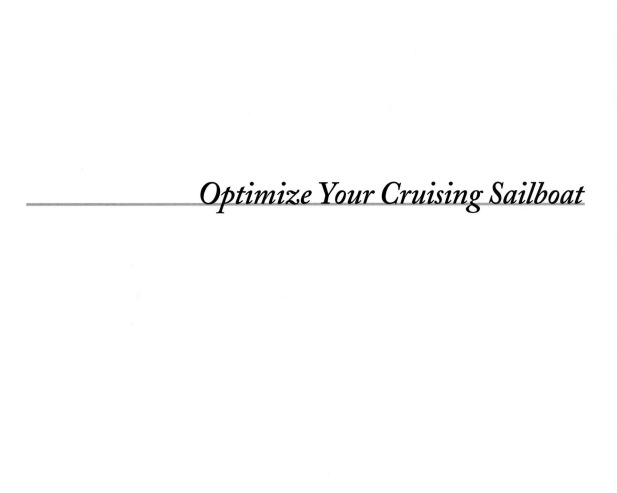

Optimize Your Cruising Sailboat

1

MAKE YOUR BOAT BETTER
The Practical Alternative

*I*t's common knowledge. Get a person to purchase his or her first boat, and before another year or two are out that first boat will be traded in on a "better" boat. It may be larger. It will certainly be different in some ways. But it will be "better." Moreover, the cycle doesn't stop there. After a few more years there will be a third boat. And a few years later possibly a fourth.

When you think about it, the pattern is understandable. Sailing and cruising are learning experiences. Usually, one of the key things learned is that features that seemed important before you had much cruising experience seem less important after several weekends or weeks of actual cruising. In other words, you look at your boat needs differently as a result of your newly gained experience.

For example, my wife and I originally built *Sea Sparrow*'s interior to accommodate us and our five daughters. When three of our five teenaged daughters joined us in Bermuda for a week one summer, we discovered that three vibrating teenagers and two parents on a 36-foot boat for that time period was as much as we or the boat could handle—the whole family at once would have been out of the question! The next winter, we converted the quarter-berth area to stowage, and we have never missed that extra berth. We've also found that having one or two guests at a time is quite comfortable. (Berths five and six, which we still have, are pilot berths port and starboard. We use them for stowage inshore and sleeping offshore.)

Another thing you learn is that every cruising boat is a compromise. It's a compromise between comfort, accommodations, ease of sailing, seaworthiness, performance, appearance, and cost. And because every boat is a compromise, few sailors are ever completely satisfied. Hence the frequent trading up, the never-ending search for a better boat—that is, one that better satisfies the evolving needs and desires of its owner.

It needn't always work that way, however. That is, you don't necessarily have to buy a different boat to get a better one. For example, a couple we met at an Annapolis, Maryland, boatyard found what they feel is a more practical alternative. A few years ago they began to grow dissatisfied with their 1976 Pearson 26, and they started thinking about moving up to a "better" boat. They attended sailboat shows and looked at a number of new and recent-vintage used boats. But the more they looked at other boats, comparing them with their nearly 20-year-old Pearson, and the more they considered the costs involved in trading up to a "better" boat, the less certain they became.

First, they realized they didn't really want a bigger boat. They liked the size of their Pearson. Second, when they made a list of the things they didn't like about their old boat, they discovered that there were only four basic problems: they continually had problems with their old engine; they didn't like the existing head (toilet); they wanted new sails, including a furling jib; and their boat had gelcoat blisters that needed repair. "And then we realized," they said, "that we could take care of all of those things for a lot less money than we'd have to spend for another boat that probably wouldn't be as well built as this one." When we met them 4 years later, they still owned the 1976 Pearson 26. Upgrading the boat had cost a total of $8,000, but they had a boat that they knew well and that suited them and their cruising needs. They were "really happy" with their decision to make their existing boat better instead of replacing it with another boat that would have come with its own list of compromises.

And that's the idea behind this book. It isn't always, or perhaps even often, necessary to change boats to get what you want. It may be as easy as making some relatively minor or not so minor changes to your existing boat. The question is, "Will you be better served by getting a different boat or by upgrading your existing boat?"

You can answer that question by deciding how you'd like your present boat to be different, or better. What is it that you're dissatisfied with on your existing boat? Do you want more comfort? Do you want a boat that's easier to handle? Perhaps you'd like to extend your cruising range and want a more seaworthy boat. Maybe you're increasingly frustrated by your boat's sailing performance—particularly when acquaintances with some of the newer, high-tech designs leave you astern—and want a boat that sails faster. Perhaps you wish for a boat with a little more eye appeal? Or does your wish list include some elements of all of these?

Whatever you're looking for, it may not be necessary to get a different boat. Your present boat may have possibilities that you haven't considered. Obviously, if you want a bigger boat, I can't offer you a boat stretcher. But if you are satisfied with the size of your boat, I've got any number of suggestions for ways to make cruising sailboats more comfortable, easier to handle, and more seaworthy, to increase their sailing performance, and even to make them look better. In many cases, I provide rough estimates of the cost involved.

But be sure to use your imagination when considering the ideas discussed in the pages that follow. I include ideas for boats about 24 to about 45 feet long. Obviously, not all of the suggestions are suitable for all boats within that range. There should, however, be ideas here for everyone, particularly if you look at the suggestions with an eye toward how they might be adapted to fit your boat.

2

MAKE YOUR BOAT
More Comfortable

*T*he builder of your boat was working with at least two powerful constraints. First, he had to construct your boat at a cost that would make its price competitive in the marketplace. Doing so meant omitting details that would have pushed the cost beyond his target price point. (That same cost pressure has contributed to the trend toward lighter and lighter displacements.)

Second, he had to respond to the market appeal of then current design fads or trends. Over the past 20 years this has led to relatively shallow hull sections with flat runs and lighter displacements in the quest for "performance." More recently it has led many builders of cruising boats to adopt lightweight mast sections with highly tuned lightweight, multispreader rigs originally designed for racing yachts—again in the name of "performance." In most instances, this "performance" orientation has been adopted at the expense of seakindliness and, possibly, rig safety for those whose cruising plans include heading offshore.

The result is that all but a few very expensive production sailboats offer opportunity for improved comfort. And that's what this chapter is about.

Although the concept of comfort on a cruising sailboat is a moving target—there are some who would argue that no sailboat is comfortable in a seaway—I have chosen to focus on three areas in which you can increase your comfort and that of your crew. Those areas are your boat's "livability"; its "seakindliness," that is, the ease and comfort with which your boat sails in a seaway; and the sense of personal security your boat affords you and your crew while cruising. All three of these apply whether you cruise on weekends in local waters, make vacation cruises exploring waters farther afield, or live aboard your boat and cruise inland, coastal, or offshore waters the year round.

LIVABILITY

Enhancing your boat's livability involves adjusting its accommodations and facilities to meet your specific needs. It can be as simple as changing the decor below. For example, if your main saloon and sleeping cabins are finished in dark woods such as teak or mahogany, you may be surprised to find out how much the strategic use of white paint on the bulkheads and the sides of some cabinets can brighten up both your boat's interior and, more importantly, the crew's mood when you are stuck below for two or three days of cold, rainy weather. Alternatively, if your interior sometimes makes you think of a bleach bottle, I've got suggestions for relieving that shiny white gelcoat finish as well. And don't forget the cockpit since you probably spend more than half of the time you are on your boat there.

COCKPIT

While a serious racer may need a cockpit that is strictly functional, cruisers usually want a few creature comforts in the cockpit as well.

Cockpit Porthole

An opening port in the after end of the cabinhouse makes a handy communications window when the weather or sea conditions warrant keeping the companionway hatch closed. It can be used for passing a hot drink or just for conversation. On *Sea Sparrow* this porthole (a Bomar 200, which requires a 5½-by-12½-inch hole in the cabinhouse) opens to the galley. You may prefer to have it open to the nav station. In either case, it's an easy installation. If you will be sailing offshore, I recommend a cast aluminum alloy, stainless steel, or bronze frame port that can be dogged securely. If you are concerned that a port in the cabinhouse might make your cockpit seating less comfortable, have a special cushion fabricated with a hole in it for the port. Prices for bronze opening ports start at about $150. Rectangular stainless steel opening ports begin at about $250. List prices for cast almag ports such as the Bomar port begin at about $450 but may be discounted significantly by one or

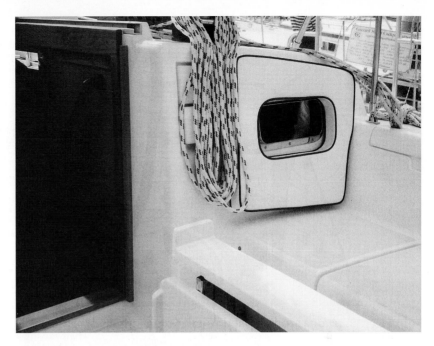

more of the major marine equipment stores. Plastic ports cost from $50 to $75 and are widely available.

To install your cockpit porthole, mark the hole to be cut using an indelible marker. Use a saber saw to make the cutout after drilling a $\frac{5}{16}$- or $\frac{3}{8}$-inch starter hole for the saber saw blade. Before installing the port, don't forget to seal the wood core of the cabinhouse laminate with at least two coats of epoxy resin. When the epoxy sealer has cured completely, install the port following the manufacturer's instructions, bedding both the port and the trim ring well with silicone or acrylic caulk.

Companionway Doors

Most cruising boats spend more time at anchor or at the dock than they do underway. And hatchboards can become inconvenient. There is an alternative, however, that lets you use hatchboards under sail and enjoy the convenience of hinged doors at all other times. Fabricate the doors to fit within the exterior teak trim around the hatchway and use pull-apart hinges (e.g., Sea Dog #204278 RH and LH hinges) to hang the doors. You can put louvers and screens in the doors for ventilation even when it is raining. You can also place the hatchboards behind the doors for added security. When you don't want to use the doors, just lift them off their hinges and put them in a locker.

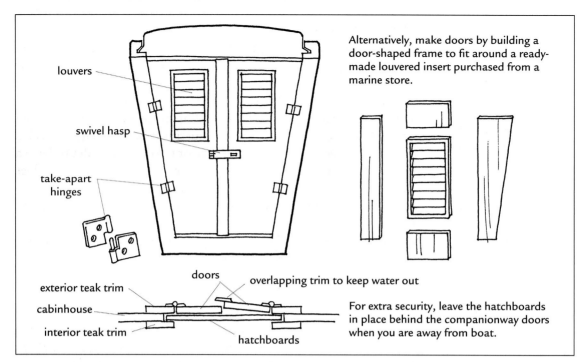

louvers

swivel hasp

take-apart hinges

Alternatively, make doors by building a door-shaped frame to fit around a ready-made louvered insert purchased from a marine store.

doors

overlapping trim to keep water out

exterior teak trim

cabinhouse

interior teak trim

hatchboards

For extra security, leave the hatchboards in place behind the companionway doors when you are away from boat.

Removable companion-way doors

Companionway Hatch Cover

If your boat is not equipped with a turtle cover (sea hood) for the sliding companionway hatch, consider providing one. If your boat demands a wood turtle cover, you should make it of teak because teak's natural oiliness will stand up well to the moisture inevitably trapped inside the hatch. If you want a fiberglass cover, you'll save money in the long run by hiring a fiberglass mechanic to make one for you. Then you can install it, bedding it well with a polyurethane adhesive-sealant such as 3M's 5200 or Sika's Sikaflex 292. Don't forget to put drains on the sides near the forward end of the hatch cover.

Companionway sliding hatch cover
The turtle hatch cover fits over the opened companionway hatch. When the sliding hatch is closed, the cover shields the forward end of the hatch, keeping water from leaking under the hatch. When installing, bed well.

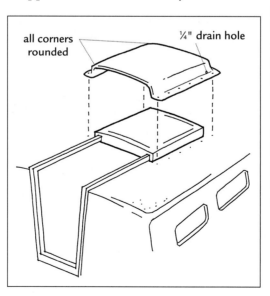

all corners rounded

¼" drain hole

Steering Wheel

On too many modern sailboats the wheel used for steering is far larger than it needs to be and makes getting around the cockpit awkward at best and dangerous at worst. You probably would find a smaller wheel easier to live with. If the helm feels too heavy, it's probably because you've got too much sail up or the sails aren't trimmed properly. Aside from style, the only justification for a large wheel is that it allows you to sit off to one side or the other in order to keep a close eye on the trim of your jib or to get a clearer view of the fleet when racing. One of the easiest ways to make your cockpit more user-friendly is to replace that monster wheel with a smaller cousin. Destroyer-style stainless steel wheels as small as 18 inches in diameter are available. Depending upon their size, smaller wheels will range in price from about $200 to $300.

Stern Rail Gate

If you have a transom ladder and have to climb over your stern rail to use it, make a gate in the top rail so that you can use the ladder more safely. By leaving the lower rail intact, you retain much of the strength and stiffness of the stern rail. A professional fabricator has more options than you do for making your gate attractive, sturdy, and easy to use—but if you want to do it yourself, you can ei-

Stern rail gate
A short section of life-line wire forms the gate, using a toggle jaw fitting at one end and a pelican hook with a spring-loaded pull-pin latching system at the other end. Drill and tap the rail ends so that they will receive machine screws in place of the usual set screws on eye caps. Use Lok-Tite or similar product to ensure screws will not work lose. Use a standard D shackle on one end cap to receive the pelican hook.

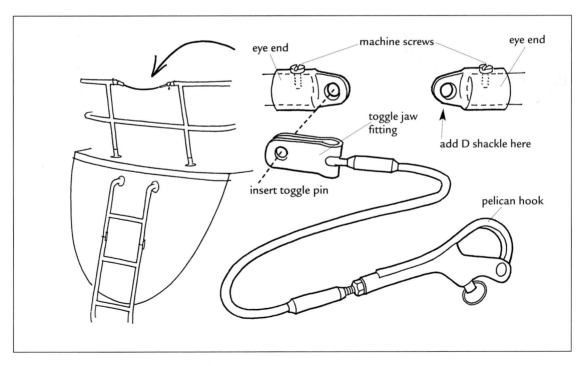

eye end · machine screws · eye end · toggle jaw fitting · add D shackle here · insert toggle pin · pelican hook

ther use a lifeline gate or adapt the stainless tube you have cut out of the top rail to serve as the gate. The necessary hardware should be available from major marine stores. When installing railing fittings, however, do not rely on set screws. Instead, drill and tap the rail to accept a machine screw in place of the set screw.

Stern Rail Seating

Some new boats are equipped with a convenience I think every aft cockpit cruising boat should have—seats tucked into the corners of the stern rail. Moreover, on many if not most boats, it's an easy add-on using ready-made seats like those sold by American Business Concepts under the brand name Stern Perch. The cost for two plain, white ready-made seats and all the hardware required for installation comes to about $200. Add about $100 for seats with blue cushions bonded to them. If you want to soften your back rest, blue tubular rail cushioning will cost about $50 per seat.

You can also make seats for your stern rail, using either ¼ teak (the finished thickness of ¼ teak is a full 1 inch) or ¾-inch marine grade plywood sealed with several coats of an epoxy resin. (If using teak, try to find a piece 12 inches wide; the alternative is joining two or more pieces to obtain the needed width.) Drill holes through the rail to receive ³⁄₁₆-inch round head machine screws (with flat washers top and bottom and lock nuts) used to fasten the seat to the rail. If the design of your seat requires a supporting leg, use 1-inch stainless steel tubing with low round bases top and bot-

Stern rail seats

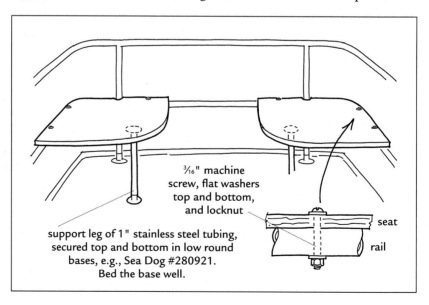

³⁄₁₆" machine screw, flat washers top and bottom, and locknut

support leg of 1" stainless steel tubing, secured top and bottom in low round bases, e.g., Sea Dog #280921. Bed the base well.

seat

rail

tom. Bed the base well where it is secured to the deck or cockpit seat. Use #12 self tapping oval-head screws to fasten the round bases to the underside of the seat and to the deck. Drill and tap the leg to receive #6 round-head stainless steel machine screws in place of set screws provided with the bases.

GALLEY

Let's face it: if a boat's galley is nothing else, it is compact. And most boatbuilders make use of every little bit of space. Or do they?

Stowage Space

When you are at anchor or cruising in protected waters, a series of hooks along the edge of the counter behind your gimbaled stove can provide a convenient place to hang your large cooking utensils— spatulas, large spoons, forks, grater, and so on. You'll need to get them out for use before you light the stove (*you should not reach over a lighted stove to get anything!*), but it sure beats digging in a locker for them.

The space over the galley sink also is usually wasted. You can correct that situation by hanging an overhead rack to hold spices and lightweight cups, wine glasses, and so on. If you don't already have a galley grab pole from your countertop to the overhead to anchor one end of your rack, consider installing one (see Keeping Crew Safe below Deck in chapter 4). Besides providing a handy anchor for your galley rack, it makes moving about the cabin in a seaway much easier. If you don't have a galley grab pole and don't want one, hang your galley rack from the overhead and anchor the outboard end to the side of the cabinhouse.

Cooking utensil stowage
Brass screw hooks hold the utensils.

Galley Rack Hung from Overhead

1. Make end and top pieces of ¾" teak.
2. Make middle and bottom shelves of ½" teak.
3. Make middle vertical braces by ripping ½" strip from ¾" teak. Braces will be ½" thick by ¾" wide.
4. Notch end pieces to receive ½" middle shelf.
5. Drill and prefit all pieces. Install screws just far enough to hold unit together.
6. Hold unit in place and mark location of two top pieces on the overhead.
7. Disassemble rack.
8. Glue and screw top pieces to overhead.
9. Assemble rack in place, gluing and screwing all joints.

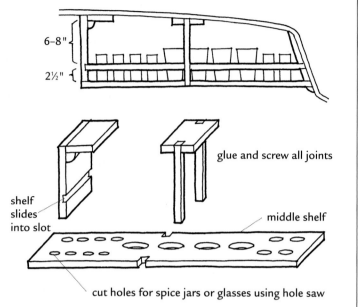

6–8"

2½"

glue and screw all joints

shelf slides into slot

middle shelf

cut holes for spice jars or glasses using hole saw

Rack Anchored to Grab Pole

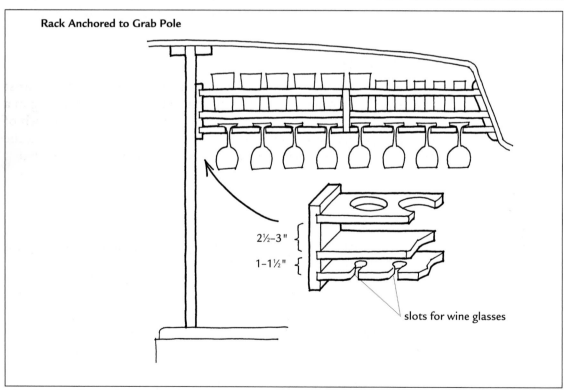

2½–3"

1–1½"

slots for wine glasses

Overhead galley rack—two versions

Work Space

You may be able to add a couple of feet of counter space to the galley quickly and easily by making a wood top for your stove. One way is simply to purchase a large wood cutting board and cut it down as needed so that it will rest atop your burners, fitting a little loosely within your stove's side rails. You'll also need to drill a finger hole so that you can get the board out easily when you want to use the burners.

Another way is to adapt a wood tray to fit on top of your stove's rails. To keep the tray securely in place, fasten ¾-by-½-inch strips of wood on the underside so that they fit just inside the stove rails. If you can't find a ready-made tray, a piece of veneered plywood, then four pieces of ¾-by-½-inch teak long enough to fit around the outside edge of your tray and a good adhesive are all you'll need to make one. Of course, you'd still need to add pieces to the bottom of a tray to hold it in place on the stove.

HEAD

The head may be one of the smallest spaces on your boat, but it's also one of the most important from the perspective of convenience and comfort.

Toilet Lid

Few things are more annoying than a toilet lid that falls against your back when you are trying to use the head while sailing in a seaway or heeled to the wrong side. Simply running a length of shock cord between two eye straps secured to the wall behind the toilet will solve the problem. Just pull the shock cord over the open lid to hold it securely in place. Use figure-eight knots in the ends of the shock cord.

Towels

Towel bars waste space in a cruising boat's head. Moreover, unless you use clothespins to hold them in place, towels have a bad habit of slipping off towel bars when the boat is underway. Instead, install a series of single brass hooks (available inexpensively at any home supply store) near the top of the head wall and sew a sturdy loop at the midpoint of one end of your towels so that you can hang them on the hooks. If you mount a piece of ¾-by-2-inch teak at the top of the bulkhead and screw the hooks to the teak rather than fastening them directly to the bulkhead, the towels will hang out a bit from the wall and dry more easily. You can do the same for washcloths, installing the hooks, for example, above and to the side of the wash basin.

To keep towels from swinging about in a rough sea, tuck them behind a length of shock cord strung between two eye straps fastened to the bulkhead about 3 feet below the hooks. You'll be able to hang more towels in the same space, *and* they'll stay put.

INTERIOR DECOR

Modern production techniques usually dictate the use of a fiberglass hull liner, with the result that interior "walls" (or sections of those "walls") along the hull of your cruising boat may be of shiny white fiberglass—easy to keep clean but short on visual warmth.

Covering Your Hull Liner

With a little bit of work, you can convert a shiny fiberglass surface to a warm wood surface by using strips of white ash 1½ inch wide by ¼ inch thick to cover the fiberglass. If the fiberglass of the hull liner is too thin to hold screws securely, stainless steel pop rivets will do nicely for fastening the wood strips to the liner. In addition, a thin coating of acrylic or silicone caulk on the underside of the wood will help secure the strips to the fiberglass but still allow you to remove them if necessary in the future. Any excess caulk that squeezes out from under the wood can be cleaned up easily with a wet rag if you apply a coat of clear finish to the wood strips before installing them.

Working from the top, fit and predrill the screw or rivet holes in the first strip of ash and in the hull liner. Double-check the fit using small-diameter nails to align all of the holes while you hold the ash securely in place. When you're satisfied with the fit, apply caulk to the back of the ash and install the first strip, working from one end to the other. (This will probably require a second pair of hands.) With the topmost strip in place, repeat the process strip by strip, leaving about ⅛ inch between strips. If necessary, trim the bottom strip to a narrower width to make it fit. Note: Although I suggest a space of ⅛ inch between strips of ash, the amount of space you leave should be what is pleasing to your eye. The space should be uniform, however.

If the hull liner will take screws, use #8 self-tapping oval head stainless steel screws, countersinking the screws only until the edge of the screw head is flush with the wood surface. Leave the screw heads exposed. If you use pop rivets, consider countersinking the rivets ⅛ inch and using wood plugs to cover the rivet heads. You can make your own ash plugs with a small drill press and a plug-cutting bit. Use white glue to secure the plugs, then sand them using a wood

1. Measure vertical height and divide by 1½" to determine the number of strips of wood needed.
2. Start with ¾ ash board long enough to provide the lengths needed.
3. Cut required number of strips ¼" thick.
4. Use sander or router to round off (bullnose) outer edges.
5. Apply sealer coat of clear acrylic or urethane finish on all surfaces of each strip.
6. Fit pieces, starting from top. Predrill holes for screws or pop rivets in first strip of ash and in hull liner. Use small-diameter nails as pins to hold ash in place as holes are drilled. If hull surface is flat, drill holes at 15–18" intervals (minimum two per strip). If bending is required, drill holes closer together.
7. Apply thin layer of silicone or acrylic caulk to back of first ash strip.
8. Install the strip, working from one end to the other to put in fasteners. Use small nails to help hold strip in position while putting in screws or pop rivets.
9. Repeat steps 6–8 until last strip is installed.
10. Plug holes if pop rivets are used. Apply 4–5 coats of clear finish (not shown).

Adding wood to your cabin liner

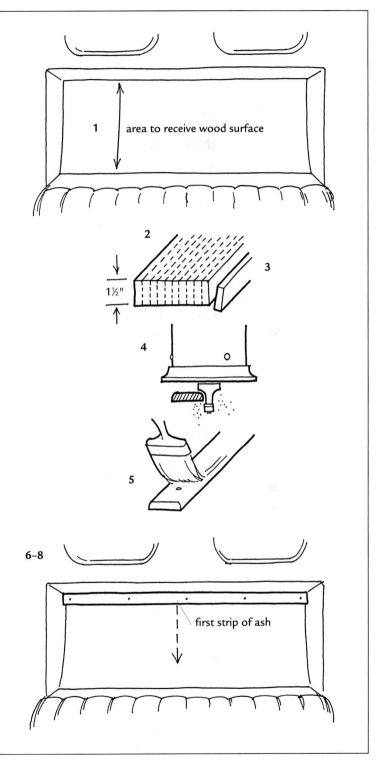

1 area to receive wood surface

2

3

1½"

4

5

6–8

first strip of ash

Bulkhead window

block to bring them flush with the wood surface. After you apply a few coats of water-base clear polyurethane coating, the job is finished. I recommend the clear polyurethane finish because varnish will darken with time.

Opening Up the Interior

Do you ever get that "closed in" feeling on a rainy day spent down below? You may be able to increase the sense of space in your main cabin by creating a window in the bulkhead separating the main cabin from your forward sleeping cabin. Leave a minimum of 6 inches of bulkhead on all sides of the window, then trim the opening with teak and install solid or louvered panels so that you can close off the sleeping cabin when needed. Louvered doors will enhance ventilation; you can buy components for making them from many marine outlets.

LIGHTING

In the evening, or when you're hunkered down below on a rainy day, it's nice to be able to read. But reading requires good lighting—something many cruising boats lack.

Fluorescent Cabin Lights

You can greatly improve your cabin lighting—and reduce the drain on your boat's batteries—by replacing 12-volt incandescent lights with fluorescent lights designed for your boat's 12-volt system. I recommend the fluorescent lights sold by Alpenglow. They are miserly with electricity but provide outstanding light. The overhead lights are available with red bulbs to safeguard night vision as well. Because they are pricey compared with other cabin lights—about $100—we opted to install them only in the galley and the main cabin. We retained the dimmer incandescent lights in the head and forward cabin. Alpenglow also has modified a standard marine reading light for use with a special fluorescent bulb that provides better light for reading while consuming even less electricity than their overhead lights.

SPACE

Space is always at a premium on a cruising boat. However, boatbuilders seem to think that sailors want to sleep an army and that they need large clothes closets. There is opportunity in these two contradictions.

From Hanging Locker to Shelf Space

Hanging lockers save boatbuilders money but often waste space for boatowners. You can increase your stowage space significantly by installing shelves in the hanging locker (see drawing page 18). If the locker is particularly deep, you may be able to have the best of both worlds—shelves outboard along the hull for things you don't often need and a hanging locker inboard. To keep gear on your shelves, drill ¼-inch holes at 5-inch intervals along the front edge of the shelves and string ³⁄₁₆-inch shock cord vertically through the holes. The shock cord will hold gear on the shelves when the boat heels but can be easily pushed aside when you want to get something out. Use ½-inch plywood for the shelves, sealing the edges with epoxy, and use ½-inch teak bulkhead molding (available from major marine stores) to trim the front edge of the shelves.

From Stateroom to Storeroom

Quarterberth storeroom

After you've had your boat for a while, you'll know which berths you use for sleeping and which ones go unused. When we found that we

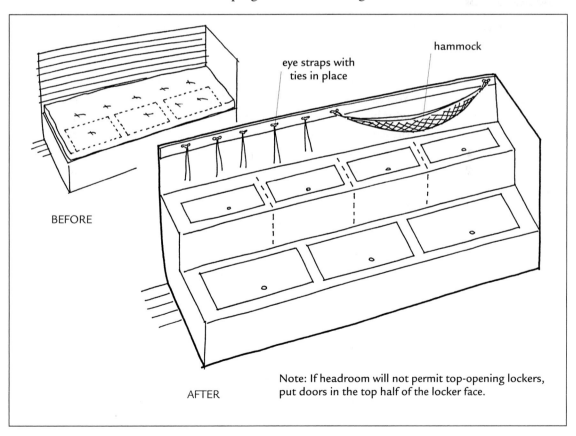

BEFORE

eye straps with ties in place

hammock

AFTER

Note: If headroom will not permit top-opening lockers, put doors in the top half of the locker face.

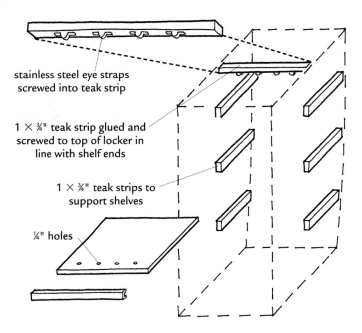

stainless steel eye straps
screwed into teak strip

1 × ¾" teak strip glued and
screwed to top of locker in
line with shelf ends

1 × ¾" teak strips to
support shelves

¼" holes

When installing shelves, bed them with a polyurethane adhesive-sealant. After the adhesive-sealant has cured, thread the ³⁄₁₆" shock cord from under the bottom shelf up through the holes to the eye strap, across the top to the next eye strap, down through the holes, and so on. Then tie a figure-eight knot in one end of the cord and work all the slack through the system, tensioning the cord a bit as you go. Stretch out the last section of shock cord and tie a figure-eight knot in that end as well. Cut ends, leaving a 2" tail at each figure-eight knot.

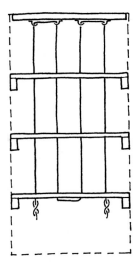

Adding shelf space to hanging lockers

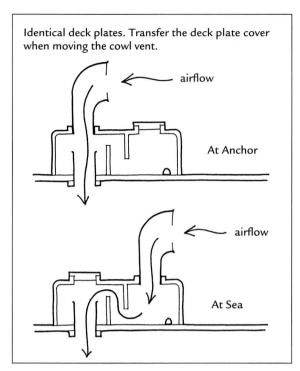

Identical deck plates. Transfer the deck plate cover when moving the cowl vent.

airflow

At Anchor

airflow

At Sea

Improving ventilation below deck

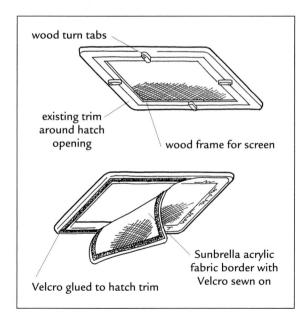

wood turn tabs

existing trim around hatch opening

wood frame for screen

Velcro glued to hatch trim

Sunbrella acrylic fabric border with Velcro sewn on

Overhead hatch screens

wouldn't be using *Sea Sparrow*'s quarter berth, we converted it to storage space by adding three top-opening lockers along the outboard portion of the berth, making sure that we still had access to the lockers under the berth. We also added eye straps on the hull liner above the new stowage lockers and along the engine box inboard, which we have used for hanging a variety of gear. Alternatively, we could hang nylon gear hammocks, also called "cargo nets," from those eye straps.

VENTILATION

The three times you most need ventilation are the times most boats are poorly equipped to provide it: when biting insects are out, when there's no breeze, and when it's raining. Even when there's a light breeze extra ventilation can make a big difference in comfort.

Dorade Vents

If your boat has one or more Dorade vents, you may be able to increase the airflow when at anchor or at a dock by installing a second deck plate on the Dorade box. In normal use, the air flowing through a Dorade vent must go under and over baffles designed to keep out water. These baffles also obstruct airflow. By installing the second deck plate directly over the opening into the cabin, you can shift the ventilator when you're at anchor or dockside so that it feeds air directly into or out of the cabin. If a rain comes up, you can just turn the cowl vent away from the rain to keep it out of the cabin.

Protection from Insects

Overhead hatch screens and a companionway screen (see Security, page 30) are a big help when insects are out. You should also have screens for any Dorade vents. Serendipitously, we also discovered on *Sea Sparrow* that the red interior lights intended to protect our night vision also help keep biting insects at bay. The red lights seem not to attract biting insects, so that fewer strays find their way into the cabin.

Power Ventilators

When there is no breeze or your hatches are snugged down against the rain, a Nicro solar-powered mushroom ventilator can make the difference between comfort and discomfort. A rechargeable battery will power the fan continuously, and the mushroom design effectively keeps out even the hardest rain. If you sail in big waters, I recommend the Nicro ventilator, model N20504BRS, which runs about $325. A threaded bronze deck plate comes with the ventilator. When you remove the ventilator and install the deck plate, your cabintop or foredeck will be secure. The less expensive ventilators (about $110) snap into a standard Nicro plastic deck plate, which is fine for cruising in more protected waters. If you will have only one ventilator, I suggest putting it on the foredeck so that it will draw air from the compan-

Solar-powered ventilation

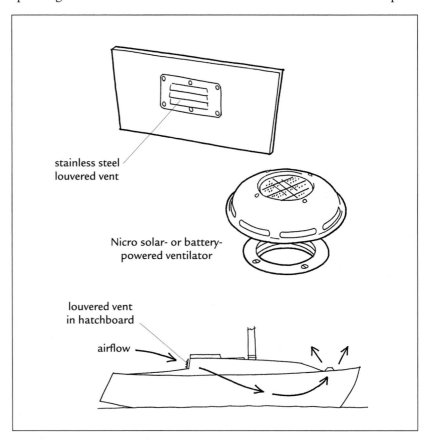

stainless steel louvered vent

Nicro solar- or battery-powered ventilator

louvered vent in hatchboard

airflow

ionway all the way through the forward cabin. (Natural ventilation on a boat generally is from the aft forward.)

To increase the airflow when your boat is completely closed up, install a small ventilating grille with a piece of nylon screen in your top hatchboard. The ventilator will then draw air throughout the entire cabin. On a boat with a center cockpit a second ventilator in the aft cabinhouse, above the berth, can be used to draw air into the cabin. If the head is not vented, consider installing one of these ventilators there as well. The Nicro ventilator comes with two different fan blades. Depending upon which blade you install, the ventilator will either pull air out or push air in. Nicro ventilators are widely available at marine stores, but you'll probably have to special order the one I've recommended for offshore use.

WATER SYSTEM

On large boats, dockside water often can be connected directly to the boat's potable-water system so that you don't deplete the supply of water in the tanks while in a marina. Being tied into a dockside water supply, however, has a potential downside if you have a failure anywhere in your boat's potable-water system. That is, your boat can sink.

Shoreside Water-Flow Regulator

If your boat is dockside and connected to a dockside water supply, install a regulator designed for use with a garden hose and lawn sprinkler (e.g., the Melnor Automatic Water Timer, which costs about $10 at home supply stores) between the shoreside water faucet and your boat. Then set the regulator to shut off the water flow after 100 or 150 gallons. That way, no more than 100 or 150 gallons of water can flood into your boat in the event of a failed hose or hose clamp. Without such a regulator (or unless you turn the shoreside water off every time you leave the boat), a system failure that would simply drain your water tank if you were out sailing could sink the boat when at the dock. Note: these regulators are called "timers," but in fact they measure water flow.

SEAKINDLINESS

Although the basic characteristics affecting seakindliness are fixed in each boat's design, how you equip, load, and handle your boat can have a big effect both on how comfortably your boat sails and on how comfortably it lies at anchor. For example, shifting weight from the ends (bow and stern) toward the middle tends to reduce the fore-and-aft rocking or pitching motion often called "hobbyhorsing." For the most part, this means thinking about weight distribution as you stow your gear and stores. For example, we stow toilet paper, paper towels, spare bath towels, and so on—bulky items that don't add much weight—in lockers under the V-berth. Conversely, canned food goes amidships, in lockers under the settees.

Sometimes, however, you need to make changes in your boat or your equipment in order to reduce the weight in the ends. Some of these changes are quite simple, such as keeping your fluke-style (Danforth) anchor in chocks on the cabintop instead of hanging it from the bow rail, for example, or replacing your heavy proof coil anchor chain with high-test chain, which is of similar strength but weighs less. More often, however, the changes are a bit more involved; and although individual changes may save what seems only a small amount of weight (25 or 50 pounds), the cumulative total of several changes will add up.

Before you start moving equipment around or making equipment changes, however, take the time to find out just how sensitive your boat is to shifts in weight fore and aft. You can do this easily by taking your boat out for a short motoring excursion, lashing the tiller or locking the wheel to steer the boat in a straight line while you are standing (hands off) at the helm. Then leave the helm and walk up to the bow, watching to see what, if any, effect your moving about the boat has on the course steered. If you can go up and sit on the bow rail while your boat chugs merrily along in a straight line, then you'll probably have to move quite a bit more than your body weight to affect your boat's motion. If, however, the course does change, you know that the equivalent of your weight definitely affects the boat's trim and, therefore, its motion. You can also conclude that getting whatever weight you can out of the ends will reduce pitching.

Dinghy Stowage

Dinghy davits have become increasingly popular for lifting the ship's boat out of the water. They are great whether you are using your dinghy daily or are in a marina and not using it at all. If you'll be sailing in a seaway, however, stowing your dinghy on deck will get that weight away from the stern and help reduce the fore-and-aft rocking motion.

To stow your hard dinghy on deck, install wood chocks and either U-bolts, folding padeyes, or fixed padeyes—with backing plates—

Inflatable

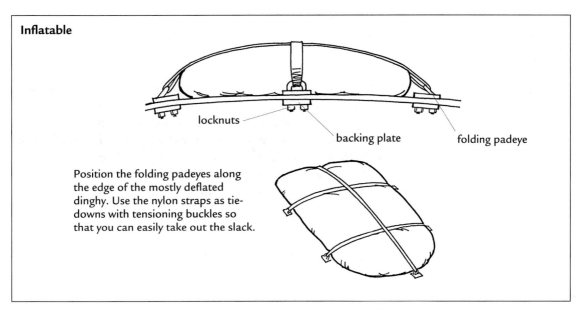

locknuts ··········· backing plate folding padeye

Position the folding padeyes along the edge of the mostly deflated dinghy. Use the nylon straps as tie-downs with tensioning buckles so that you can easily take out the slack.

Hard dinghy

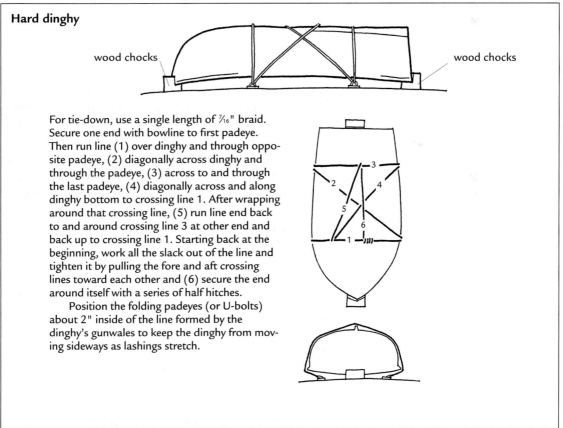

wood chocks ········· wood chocks

For tie-down, use a single length of ⁷⁄₁₆" braid. Secure one end with bowline to first padeye. Then run line (1) over dinghy and through opposite padeye, (2) diagonally across dinghy and through the padeye, (3) across to and through the last padeye, (4) diagonally across and along dinghy bottom to crossing line 1. After wrapping around that crossing line, (5) run line end back to and around crossing line 3 at other end and back up to crossing line 1. Starting back at the beginning, work all the slack out of the line and tighten it by pulling the fore and aft crossing lines toward each other and (6) secure the end around itself with a series of half hitches.

Position the folding padeyes (or U-bolts) about 2" inside of the line formed by the dinghy's gunwales to keep the dinghy from moving sideways as lashings stretch.

Easy deck stowage for dinghies

on your cabinhouse or foredeck so that you can carry the dinghy bottomside up. Put down the bow and transom chocks first, arranging them so that the chocks keep the bow and stern about 1 inch off the deck and prevent the dinghy from moving forward or backward. With the dinghy in place, mark positions for the tie-down fittings *inside* the gunnels. This way, the lashings will more effectively keep the dinghy from moving sideways than if the tie-downs were directly in line with or outboard of the gunnels. You'll need to tighten the lashings regularly when they're in use because the rope will stretch, but that's easy to do: simply tighten the lashing between the forward and aft tie-downs.

For stowing your inflatable on deck, use folding padeyes, one each at the bow and stern and two for each side. These too must have backing plates. It's best to avoid the temptation to use the dinghy as a handy storage box; instead, stow it bottomside up and partially deflated under your lashings. Use nylon strapping for your lashings rather than rope to minimize potential chafing problems.

Lazarettes

On many boats, the lazarette takes on the characteristics of a garage, basement, or attic ashore: it gets crammed with stuff—all of which weighs down your stern and much of which is never used because it's buried and forgotten. Since human nature is to fill such spaces, our solution on *Sea Sparrow* was to make the lazarette smaller by installing a removable shelf that cut the locker's depth almost in half. True, the area under that shelf goes unused, but that shelf has made our lazarette much more user-friendly because we can reach every corner. Most of the volume that's now under the shelf was impossible to reach anyway without hanging practically upside down, and we don't miss it a bit.

Stern Gear

Many kinds of equipment have been developed to make cruising easier, but many of these are mounted on the stern. Dinghy davits, radar and antenna posts and platforms, solar-panel mounts, and hoists for lifting outboard motors and other heavy gear from dinghy to deck are but some examples. Few of these, however, must be on the stern when you go to sea. For example, dinghy davits and motor hoists can be installed in such a way that they can be removed easily for stowage below deck. Examples include the St. Croix Removable Davit System, the Forespar Motor Mate lifting davit, and the St. Croix Little Crane motor hoist.

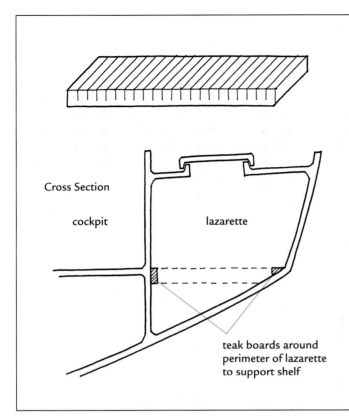

Cross Section

cockpit

lazarette

teak boards around
perimeter of lazarette
to support shelf

1. To bend ¾ × 2" teak boards to fit
   the hull contour, make a series of
   cuts ½" deep across boards at ½"
   intervals.
2. Install boards with cuts toward
   the hull, using an excess of polyurethane adhesive-sealant. If you
   cannot glue and screw the strips
   (e.g., if you don't want to put
   screws into solid fiberglass-
   reinforced plastic laminate),
   wedge strips in place with other
   pieces of wood until the adhesive-
   sealant has cured.
3. With perimeter boards in place,
   make cardboard templates for
   shelf boards, remembering that
   you have to fit the shelf boards
   through the lazarette hatch. Use
   ¾" plywood for shelves. When
   shelf boards are in place, secure
   them with screws.

Adding a lazarette shelf

Nor do solar panels have to be mounted on arches across the stern. Solar panels can be safely and effectively hung from your lifelines just forward of the stern rail or from stainless steel bars installed just below the upper lifeline between the stern rail and the first lifeline stanchion. Rigged in this manner, *Sea Sparrow*'s solar panels have safely weathered gale-force winds and seas during thousands of offshore cruising miles.

Solar panels can also be mounted safely on your cabinhouse, hard dodger, or pilothouse—even in work areas—by providing a sturdy protective covering. The most effective protection is a stainless steel frame supporting a ⅜-inch clear Lexan polycarbonate cover. In designing the cover, however, leave at least a ½-inch air space between the solar panel and the Lexan to prevent overheating. In addition, the inside of the stainless steel frame should measure 2 inches wider and longer than the solar panel so that the frame will not cast shadows on the panel.

I've also seen stainless steel grilles that provide excellent protection for the solar panels. However, the shadows cast on the panel by the grille will reduce the panels' efficiency by an estimated 20 percent or more.

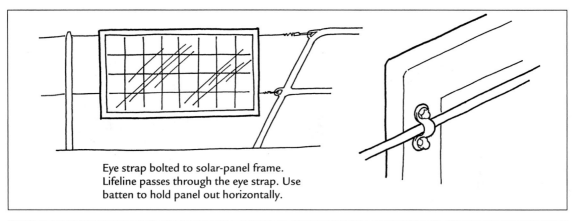

Eye strap bolted to solar-panel frame.
Lifeline passes through the eye strap. Use
batten to hold panel out horizontally.

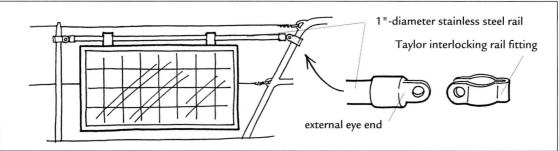

1"-diameter stainless steel rail

Taylor interlocking rail fitting

external eye end

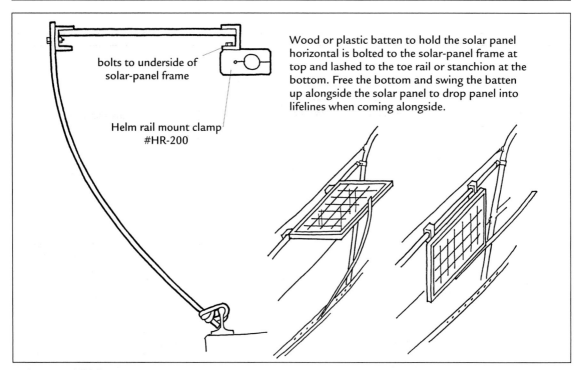

bolts to underside of
solar-panel frame

Wood or plastic batten to hold the solar panel
horizontal is bolted to the solar-panel frame at
top and lashed to the toe rail or stanchion at the
bottom. Free the bottom and swing the batten
up alongside the solar panel to drop panel into
lifelines when coming alongside.

Helm rail mount clamp
#HR-200

Solar-panel lifeline mounts

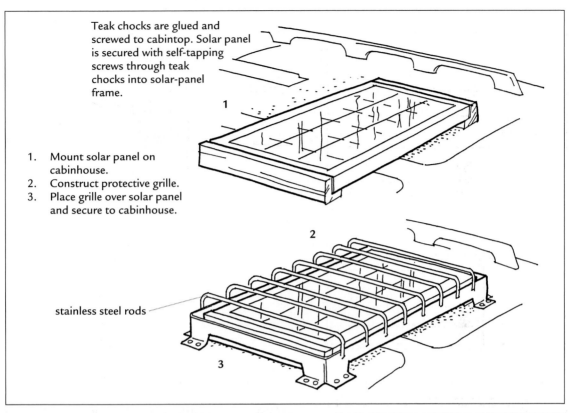

Teak chocks are glued and screwed to cabintop. Solar panel is secured with self-tapping screws through teak chocks into solar-panel frame.

1

1. Mount solar panel on cabinhouse.
2. Construct protective grille.
3. Place grille over solar panel and secure to cabinhouse.

2

stainless steel rods

3

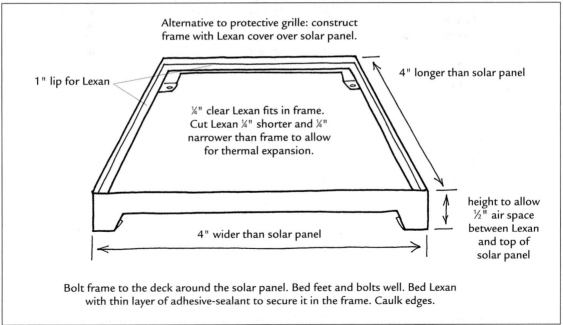

Alternative to protective grille: construct frame with Lexan cover over solar panel.

1" lip for Lexan

4" longer than solar panel

¼" clear Lexan fits in frame. Cut Lexan ¼" shorter and ¼" narrower than frame to allow for thermal expansion.

4" wider than solar panel

height to allow ½" air space between Lexan and top of solar panel

Bolt frame to the deck around the solar panel. Bed feet and bolts well. Bed Lexan with thin layer of adhesive-sealant to secure it in the frame. Caulk edges.

Cabintop solar-panel mounts

If you want your radar unit near the stern rather than on the mast, mounting it on the backstay will take some weight off the end of your boat. You can also have the radar unit gimbaled so that you have a constant, complete display at all times, even in rough conditions. Moreover, although the backstay mount is only a few feet forward of the stern rail, the change is beneficial. Think about the times you've been on a seesaw with someone who weighed less than you. By sliding forward a couple of feet on your end of the seesaw, you could balance the effect of your weight with that of your partner's lighter weight. The effect of moving your radar unit from a sternpost to the backstay is the same though certainly not so dramatic. (For additional information about radar mounts, see Guarding against Collision in chapter 4.) Another consideration when choosing both your radar system and your mounting system is the weight of the equipment. All other things being equal, choose the lightest.

Of course, boats not only rock from fore to aft; they also roll from side to side. In fact, one of the disadvantages of modern cruising boats, with their flatter hull sections and lightweight, racing-style rigs, is their typically quick rolling motion compared with that of more traditional cruising yachts, with their deeper hull sections and heavier rigs. It's one of the compromises made on behalf of improved performance.

While you can't, of course, change your hull's shape, it is possible to increase your boat's stability—and by this I mean its resistance to rolling—by replacing the mast and standing rigging with sturdier stuff. A stouter (i.e., heavier) mast section and heavier standing rigging will add weight aloft, increasing the boat's moment of inertia and, therefore, its resistance to rolling. Alternatively, you can add weight aloft by changing over to a roller-furling mainsail (see Mainsails in chapter 3). In either case, the result will be a somewhat slower, longer rolling motion and, with that, increased comfort. Even if your cruising sailboat has more traditional deep sections, adding weight aloft will increase its roll resistance. Perhaps more importantly, if you will be making serious ocean passages, the added weight aloft will increase your boat's resistance to being rolled completely in dangerously large seas.

As with any change you make to your boat, installing a heavier rig also involves compromise. The increased weight aloft will make the boat heel more easily, and you may have to reduce sail a little sooner when the wind pipes up than you did with your old, lighter rig. But your boat will be more stable, and it won't roll as easily or as quickly at anchor or underway. As an added benefit, the slower motion may help crew who have a tendency toward mal de mer. A quick rolling motion is more likely to contribute to seasickness.

One word of caution: although most cruising boats in the 24-to-45-foot range should be able to handle the extra weight of a roller-furling mainsail or heavier standing rigging, adding weight aloft will have an impact on the boat's righting moment and, therefore, on its limit of positive stability. While this may be of minimal importance if your cruising will be limited to protected or semi-protected coastal and inland waters, it could become critical if you plan to sail on the world's oceans, its major seas, or the Great Lakes.

The limit of positive stability, or LPS, defines the angle to which a boat can be rolled and still come back up onto its feet. Rolled beyond that angle, it will turn upside down. At that point, however, the important question becomes how long it will remain upside down before coming back upright. Here too the LPS is critical because the lower the LPS, the longer the boat is likely to remain upside down. In the judgment of many experts, the minimum LPS for a boat that will be sailing in offshore waters is 120 degrees. If your boat's LPS is marginal, adding weight aloft may not be advisable.

(For additional information about the role of the rig in helping a boat resist capsizing and about the importance of a boat's LPS, see the Technical Committee of the Cruising Club of America report in *Desirable and Undesirable Characteristics of Offshore Yachts*, edited by John Rousmaniere, W. W. Norton, 1987. While the entire book is probably of interest mainly to professional sailors and yacht designers, pages 61–62, 67–68, and 78–79, in particular, are related to the stability issues discussed here.)

To find out your boat's LPS, go first to the builder. If the builder can't answer your question, go to the boat's designer. The designer should be able to provide the information, though you may have to pay a fee for it. Failing that, contact U.S. Sailing (see the appendix). Their files of International Measurement System (IMS) racing certificates include measurements for hundreds of different boats, and they may have measurements from a sister boat of yours. If not, the U.S. Sailing staff can refer you to a measurer who will run an inclination test on your boat and make the measurements required to calculate the LPS. U.S. Sailing can then run the calculations and give you an "experimental" certificate that would include the LPS. The cost for all of this would probably be less than $500. A full IMS racing certificate would be about $200 more.

SECURITY

I'm concerned here with two kinds of security: boat and crew safety, that is, having a boat that is safe for the use you make of it; and personal security, that is, feeling safe from intrusions by the outside world. You may legitimately ask what these have to do with comfort. The answer is, Everything!

On a boat, just as in one's home ashore, at least two levels of comfort must be provided for: physical comfort and psychological or emotional comfort. The suggestions here related to security have to do with psychological or emotional comfort.

Both you and your crew must feel confident that your boat will take care of you and that it's equipped so that you can take care of yourself. You gain this confidence as you acquire experience with your boat in different sailing conditions and by making improvements as necessary to provide for your safety. If you don't have that confidence in your boat, the emotional stresses involved in dealing with difficult conditions can ruin your cruise. The same statement applies to your own and your crew's sense of security when anchored or tied up in a strange marina. If you or any of your crew members are concerned about the possibility of dealing with an intruder on the boat, your cruise will be anything but relaxing. There are suggestions in this chapter related to both boat safety and personal security when cruising in inland or coastal waters. Suggestions related to offshore sailing are found in chapter 4.

BOAT AND CREW SAFETY

A series of small, inexpensive improvements will go a long way toward enhancing boat and crew safety and your subsequent sense of security.

Cockpit Grabrails

An important part of boat safety is having something to hold onto when standing in the cockpit or going out of the cockpit to work on deck. A handrail welded to the trailing edge of your dodger frame makes a user-friendly addition—out of the way but convenient to grab. Similarly, railings mounted on both sides of the dodger frame will give the crew something to hold on to from the time they leave the cockpit until they can reach the handrail on the cabinhouse.

1. Determine exactly where handles will be mounted.
2. Mark spots on dodger canvas and dodger frame at the same time.
3. Remove dodger and have holes made to accommodate handles.
4. Reinstall dodger and mark places to drill holes in dodger frame.
5. Drill holes in frame and install handles. Note: It may be easier to drill holes if frame is removed from boat. When drilling holes in stainless steel, it is easier to make small holes first, then use progressively larger drill bits to reach the desired size.

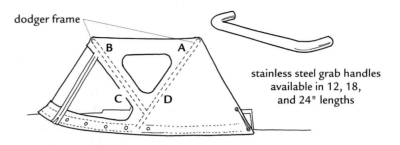

dodger frame

stainless steel grab handles available in 12, 18, and 24" lengths

There are three ways to rig a handle on the side of your dodger frame: A to B, B to C, and A to D.

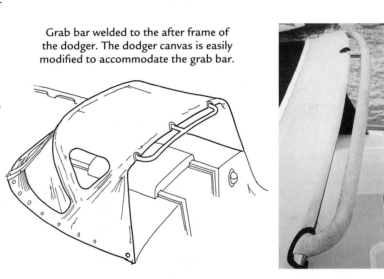

Grab bar welded to the after frame of the dodger. The dodger canvas is easily modified to accommodate the grab bar.

Dodger grabrails

Lifelines

Safety also means having lifelines adequate to keep people and sails on deck. If your boat has only a single lifeline, consider adding a second wire halfway up from the deck (see drawing page 32). You may be able to use your existing stanchions. Schaefer Marine makes a double stanchion ring (SCH-36-04)—also called a "middle bracket"—that slips over the stanchion and locks in place with a set screw to provide a guide for a mid-height lifeline. The list price is about $25. If the ring will not fit your stanchion, it will fit a Schaefer stanchion (SCH-36-07), which lists for about $60.

Along the same line, a number of boats have lifelines that lead down to the deck at the bow to allow room for a deck-sweeping genoa. Most boats I've seen whose lifelines were rigged in that way, however, had roller-furling jibs and did not need such low lifelines. For cruising

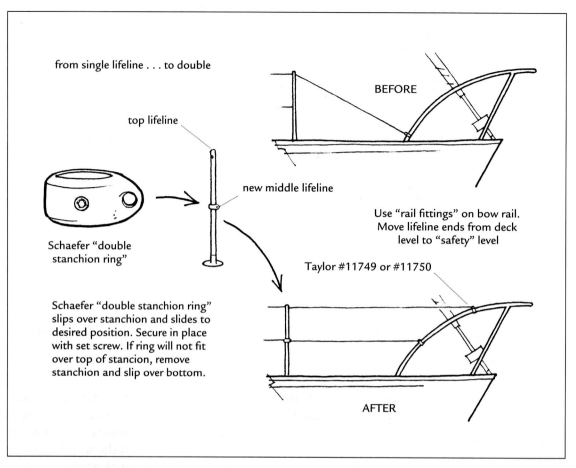

from single lifeline . . . to double

top lifeline

BEFORE

new middle lifeline

Schaefer "double stanchion ring"

Use "rail fittings" on bow rail. Move lifeline ends from deck level to "safety" level

Taylor #11749 or #11750

Schaefer "double stanchion ring" slips over stanchion and slides to desired position. Secure in place with set screw. If ring will not fit over top of stancion, remove stanchion and slip over bottom.

AFTER

Upgrading lifelines

people, those foredeck lifelines should be raised to make the foredeck safer. And it's an easy fix. Use Taylor stainless rail fittings for fastening your lifeline hardware to the bow rail (Taylor #11749 for ⅞-inch rail or #11750 for 1-inch rail).

Lifeline Gates

The lifeline gates on many boats are equipped with old-style pelican hooks secured with slides that have a bad habit of slipping off and allowing the pelican hook to open unexpectedly—not the safest system. It would be worthwhile to replace those old-style pelican hooks with newer designs that use a spring-loaded pin to secure the hook.

And while I'm on the subject of lifeline gates, if your boat has only a single wire for a gate, add a middle wire. Lifelines, like a chain, are only as secure as their weakest link. A single-wire gate is the weak link in an otherwise good double-lifeline system.

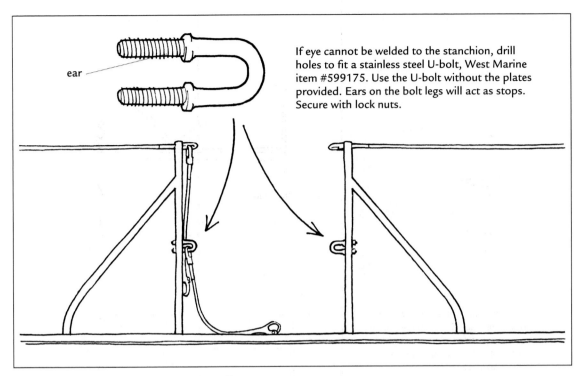

ear ....

If eye cannot be welded to the stanchion, drill holes to fit a stainless steel U-bolt, West Marine item #599175. Use the U-bolt without the plates provided. Ears on the bolt legs will act as stops. Secure with lock nuts.

Doubling up lifeline gates

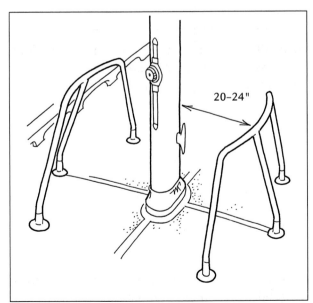

20–24"

Mast rails

Mast Rails

Mast rails, which some people call "sissy bars," are among the more important pieces of equipment on our foredeck. A mast rail on each side of the mast increases our comfort level enormously when the weather is acting up by making it much easier and safer to work at the mast while under sail—especially in a seaway. Planting your feet on the deck and jamming your fanny firmly against the mast rail leaves both your hands free to work with the sails. Even if your halyards and reef lines lead back to the cockpit, mast rails are useful. There will be times—usually in the worst of conditions—when someone will have to help out at the mast when you are taking down or reefing sails.

I prefer three-legged mast rails. The third leg stiffens the rail enormously. The rail should be about 31 to 35 inches high, just high enough to brace the top of your thighs or the bottom of your bottom.

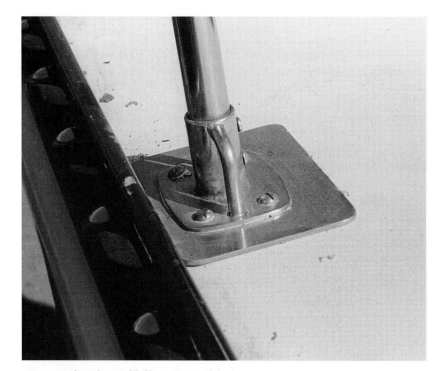

Strengthening Lifeline Stanchions

On too many modern boats lifeline stanchions are not reassuringly strong. In fact, they feel—and probably are—vulnerable. You can test yours by grabbing each stanchion and pushing in and out to see how sturdy it feels. If the stanchion base seems to wobble a bit or feels soft, check to make sure that there's a backing plate under the deck to hold the bolts securing the base. If there is not, add one that is at least the size of the stanchion base—larger if possible. If there is a backing plate, you can stiffen the stanchion by installing under it a stainless steel plate at least $\frac{1}{16}$ inch thick and 3 inches longer and 2 inches wider than the base itself. Inserted between the stanchion base and the deck, this plate will spread the load on the stanchion by giving it a larger footprint, thereby stiffening the assembly. Be sure to bed both the plate to the deck and the base to the plate well to prevent leakage.

PERSONAL SECURITY

Three strategies many people use to enhance their personal security at home ashore—exterior lighting, locks for exterior doors, and a bedside telephone or panic button—can be effective on boats as well.

Bedside Alarm

Keep a canned air horn ($12 to $45) next to your berth in a PVC horn holder (about $8). If anyone comes aboard your boat uninvited, grab the can and blow five shorts blasts—the marine danger signal—on the horn, repeating until you're certain the intruder has left. The five shorts blasts will alert your neighbors that something is afoot and undoubtedly scare your intruder away. Before you buy a horn, make sure that it will fit into the PVC horn holder. Whereas canned air horns come in different sizes, the holder appears to be available in only one size.

Securing Your Companionway

Companionway screen door and stowage rack The screen can be secured to the frame with nailing strips. Alternatively, the screen can be made with a Velcro-backed Sunbrella border. Use contact cement and stainless steel staples to fasten the Velcro mating strip to the frame.

Begin by making a hatchboard of clear acrylic sheeting (e.g., Lucite or Plexiglas) for use in place of one of your wood hatchboards. This gives you a window to the cockpit when your hatchboards are in place. For those balmy nights when you don't want to use your hatchboards, fabricate a wood-framed companionway screen to allow for ventilation. One or more crossbars in the wood frame will keep any possible intruder from cutting out the screen and slipping through your "screen door." When it's not in use, you can stow the screen door in a rack above the V-berth under the foredeck. Finally, install a wood bar that blocks the sliding hatch from opening, much like the security bars used with sliding glass doors in houses.

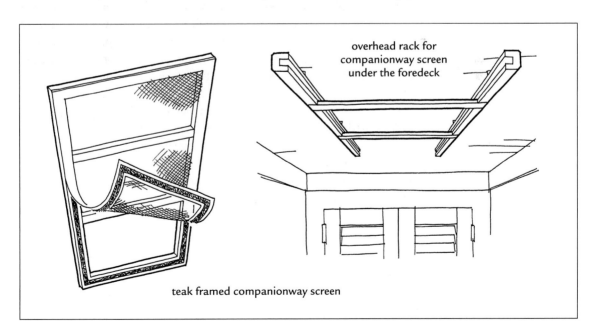

overhead rack for companionway screen under the foredeck

teak framed companionway screen

Security Lights

To make your boat unattractive to any possible nighttime intruder, rig an all-round white light that you can hang from either the bimini frame or the boom to light your cockpit. Then hang a similar light from a jib halyard about 8 feet above the foredeck. Few intruders will brave a well-lighted cockpit and foredeck.

3

MAKE YOUR BOAT
Easier to Handle

One key to cruising shorthanded successfully—that is, cruising alone or cruising as a couple alone or with young children—is to find ways to make your boat and its equipment easier to handle. We received a wonderful lesson in this when we met a 76-year-old wisp of a man single-handing on a 44-foot sloop in the Virgin Islands several years ago. He delighted in showing us some of the systems he'd adopted to compensate for his aging muscles, including one of the earliest behind-the-mast furling mainsails. With the exception of the furling mainsail, most of his ideas and homemade systems were specific to his boat and his needs, but the approach he described reverberates throughout this chapter.

At its heart is the idea of taking as much of the muscle work as is practical out of sailing, anchoring, and handling your boat. A further notion is adjusting systems so that the weakest member of the crew can handle every job—a goal that makes sense from two perspectives. First, it's a matter of safety. If the strongest member of the crew becomes incapacitated for any reason, the other crew member or members must be able to get the boat to safety. That may include single-handedly raising the anchor, raising and lowering sails, reefing sails, and bringing the boat into a dock without any help. Second, it enables all members of the crew to participate fully in sailing the boat. In other words, there are no passengers; everyone has the satisfaction of full participation. One note of caution: any time you install a labor-saving device, make sure you have a backup should the device fail. Areas in which to try to make your boat easier to handle include anchoring, running rigging, sail handling, rigging, ladders, and dinghy- and cargo-handling gear.

ANCHORING

After countless times raising and lowering anchors in waters from Maine to South and Central America, I am more convinced than ever that anchoring is more akin to art than to science. Yes, there are techniques to be learned (the science part of it), but how you apply those techniques will often determine your success or failure at anchoring, particularly when you are experiencing difficult weather conditions. However, there are ways to take some of the work out of anchoring.

ANCHOR CLEATS

On most boats, mooring cleats serve double duty for anchoring. This means leading your anchor rode either through the mooring chocks or off to the side from your bow roller to your mooring cleats to secure the rode. If your foredeck has space, there are definite advantages to installing separate, large cleats specifically for anchoring. For example, installing the cleats in line with the anchor rode leading from the bow roller will simplify securing your rode, and the straight lead will reduce the potential for chafe—a very real hazard if you are anchored during a long and strong storm. Anchor cleats are also useful if you have an all-chain rode, providing a better point for securing your chain snubber than does a mooring cleat. Finally, if the anchor cleats are located far enough forward, they may be useful for securing the shanks of your anchors when you are underway. On *Sea Sparrow* we have room for only one large anchor cleat, between the shanks of our two plow anchors. When we head offshore, we lash the two anchors to that cleat as an extra measure of security.

ANCHOR AND DECK WASHDOWN

Until you have anchored in soft, gooey mud or in nutrient-rich tropical waters where "stuff" grows on your anchor rode seemingly overnight, you may not appreciate the usefulness of a seawater washdown on the foredeck. That pressurized stream of water can save you much cleanup work and a smelly, very dirty anchor locker by enabling you to wash off the rode before it comes over your bow roller. (It once took me three hours and two toothbrushes to clean 60 feet of chain link by link.) Washdown kits range from about $80 to $230 and are relatively easy to install. Depending upon where you

Deck and anchor washdown system

The washdown pump can be mounted in the anchor or cockpit locker. Connect a garden-type hose for use. Alternatively, the pump can be stowed, brought into the cockpit or on deck when needed, and rigged for use. The closer the pump is to its power source the better.

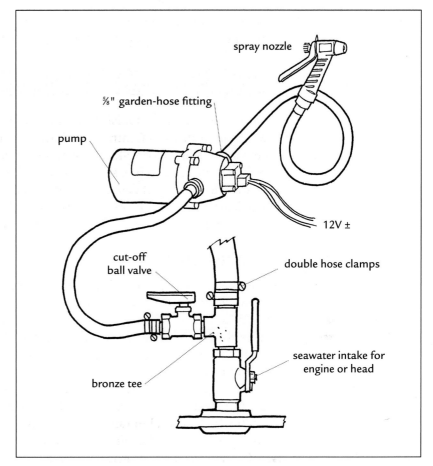

spray nozzle

⅝" garden-hose fitting

pump

12V ±

cut-off
ball valve

double hose clamps

bronze tee

seawater intake for
engine or head

mount the pump, you'll need to pay attention to the self-priming capabilities of the different pumps. Pay attention also to electrical requirements. Systems we've looked at draw from 4 to 10 amps.

ANCHOR WINDLASS

For shorthanded cruising few items of equipment are more useful than a good anchor windlass—if your boat is large enough to handle the added weight on the foredeck. (If it's not big enough to carry the extra weight, you probably don't need a windlass anyway.) We've been happy for many years with a manual Simpson Lawrence Sea Tiger two-speed windlass. If, however, the size of your boat and its electrical system will allow it, consider installing an electric windlass. For single handing, you can rig the electric windlass to be operated from the cockpit as well as from the foredeck when conditions warrant.

Note: Any powered windlass you install should have a manual backup—and many do not. So shop carefully. Without a manual

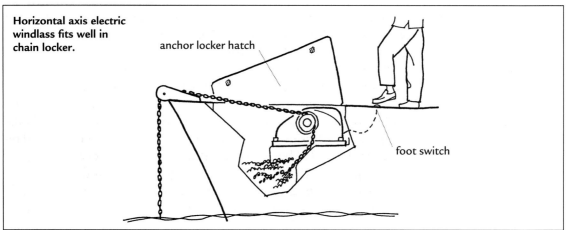

Horizontal axis electric windlass fits well in chain locker.

anchor locker hatch

foot switch

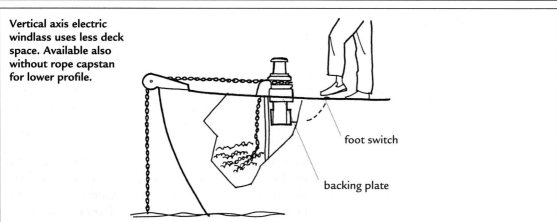

Vertical axis electric windlass uses less deck space. Available also without rope capstan for lower profile.

foot switch

backing plate

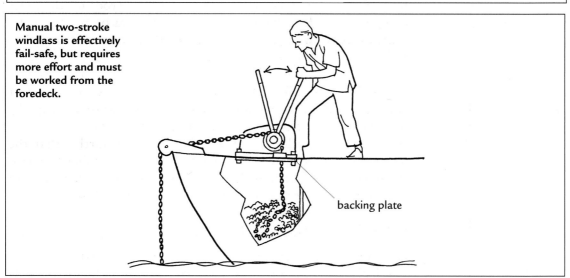

Manual two-stroke windlass is effectively fail-safe, but requires more effort and must be worked from the foredeck.

backing plate

Anchor windlasses

backup, you may not be able to get your anchor up or down when you have an electrical problem. And please note that I said *when* you have an electrical problem, not *if*.

Your anchor windlass can be mounted on deck or, possibly, inside your foredeck anchor locker. Check with the builder of your boat, however, for advice about mounting the windlass inside the locker. You'll also need to consider the path the rode (chain) will take from the windlass to your bow roller. In any case, the windlass will require some kind of backing plate, though what is needed will vary depending upon the type of windlass you select and your boat's construction. In use, when the anchor has been set, the rope rode should be cleated or the chain secured with a snubber, taking all strain off the windlass.

BOW ROLLERS

If you do not have bow rollers for your anchors, you will wonder how you did without them after installing them (see drawings page 42). If you have only one roller, a second roller will make setting two anchors much easier. Bow rollers offer one of the few good means of stowing plow, Bruce, or similar anchors. There are several things to consider, however, when adding bow rollers.

First, their sturdiness should be matched to your boat. That means that if your boat weighs between 10 and 15 tons, your bow-roller assembly should be designed and constructed to stand up to the forces it will be subject to under the worst of anchoring conditions. Second, unless you are going to take your rode off the roller and put it in a deck chock after your anchor has been set, select a roller assembly with a sturdy pin that will (1) prevent your anchor rode from jumping off the roller, (2) strengthen the side cheeks of your roller assembly so that they can't be bent out of shape by a strong sideways pull on the anchor rode, and (3) let you stow your anchor on the roller assembly should you decide to. Finally, the bow rollers should not project so far beyond the bow that they become vulnerable; ideally, they should not project farther than the bow rail. As for where to find a good bow-roller assembly, all major chandleries carry ready-made bow-roller assemblies. You might also consider having one fabricated specifically for your boat.

STERN-ANCHOR SYSTEM

For a stern anchor, stow the rode in a crate in the lazarette and install a deck plate in the coaming or afterdeck so that you can lead the rode directly from the otherwise closed lazarette through a chock and over

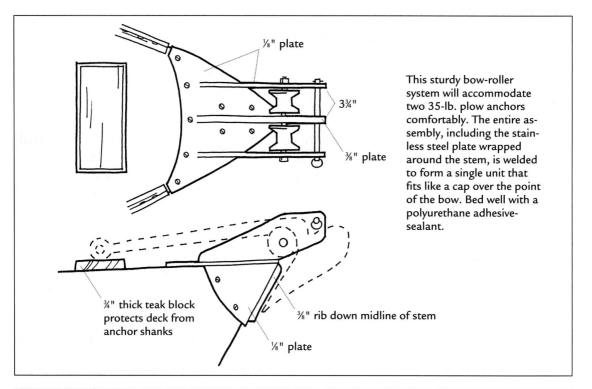

This sturdy bow-roller system will accommodate two 35-lb. plow anchors comfortably. The entire assembly, including the stainless steel plate wrapped around the stem, is welded to form a single unit that fits like a cap over the point of the bow. Bed well with a polyurethane adhesive-sealant.

⅛" plate

3¾"

⅜" plate

¾" thick teak block protects deck from anchor shanks

⅜" rib down midline of stem

⅛" plate

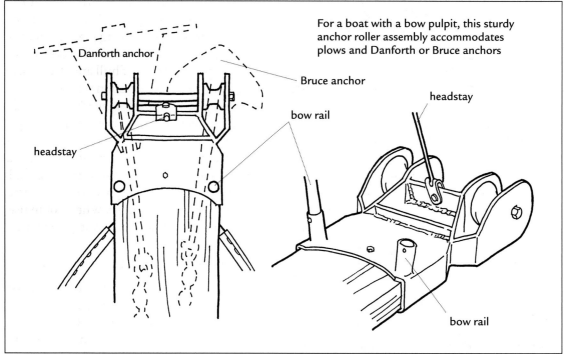

For a boat with a bow pulpit, this sturdy anchor roller assembly accommodates plows and Danforth or Bruce anchors

Danforth anchor

Bruce anchor

headstay

bow rail

headstay

bow rail

Two sturdy bow-roller assemblies

the stern. For big-water sailing I recommend using a threaded bronze or chrome-plated bronze deck plate. If room will not allow a deck plate, consider a deck pipe instead.

DOCKING

If you cruise only in local waters, docking may not be much of a challenge simply because you are docking in your home facility. As your cruising grounds expand and you start coming up to docks that are in waters with unfamiliar currents or are exposed to fresh winds, getting into a slip or alongside a dock can be more challenging.

MIDSHIP CLEATS

One of the most useful pieces of equipment for coming alongside a dock or into a slip is a midship cleat. It lets you put a spring line ashore that will hold the boat in place until you can get the bow and stern lines ashore. Unfortunately, many boats don't have midship cleats. They are another good example of a functional detail easily installed during boat construction but sacrificed by boatbuilders at the altar of cost savings.

Ideally, you would install midship mooring cleats by through-bolting them to the deck, using a good backing plate under the deck. In many modern boats, however, that's not practical. The use of hull and deck liners in modern boat construction frequently does not allow access to the underside of the deck. However, major marine stores stock or can get for you sturdy deck cleats mounted on stainless steel cars designed to fit on your genoa track. If you have a slotted aluminum toe rail, a stainless steel cleat designed to be mounted on your toe rail is available. When not in use, the toe-rail cleat folds down out of the way.

Midship cleat options

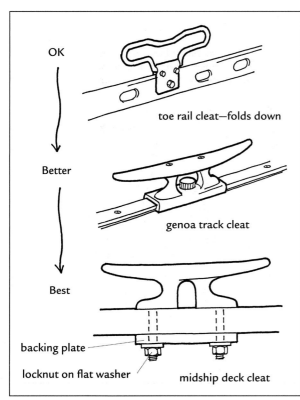

OK

toe rail cleat—folds down

Better

genoa track cleat

Best

backing plate

locknut on flat washer

midship deck cleat

FENDER HOLDERS

Coming into a dock usually means using fenders. And the larger the better. But fenders take up space. Mast rails, bow rails, stern rails, even lifeline stanchions on larger boats, may offer space to mount racks designed to hold your fenders securely. Some racks are designed to fold up so that they lie flat against the rail when not in use. Called "fender holders," these racks are readily available. If you're headed offshore, your fenders are better stowed below (you won't need them anyway), but as long as you are sailing in protected or semiprotected waters, a set of fender holders can make a lot of sense.

FUEL SYSTEM

When cruising away from your home base, there is an increased risk of buying contaminated fuel. A water separator-filter goes far toward protecting an engine from dirty fuel. Buying your fuel at facilities that do a large volume of business (including commercial business) also helps. However, one load of dirty fuel can have you changing fuel filters every few hours of engine time. For example, once, after taking on fuel while cruising in the Caribbean, we went through four filter elements in less than 20 hours of engine time before the interval between filter changes began to lengthen significantly. Fortunately, we were carrying plenty of spares. There is, however, an alternative.

FUEL-CLEANING SYSTEMS

A fuel-microbial-decontamination system that has been in use on land and sea for several years relies on a patented multiple-magnet system to destroy the microorganisms that form sludge in fuel tanks, breaking them into such small parts that they will go right through the fuel system unnoticed. Called DeBug, the system consists of a circulating pump, a magnetic unit through which the fuel circulates along a designed path around six magnets, a water separator-filter, and a timer. This system is designed so that you can periodically clean and filter all of the fuel in your tank independently of the engine. By turning a valve, you can also use the system to clean the fuel as it goes to your engine. If you don't need to be able to clean your full tank of fuel, you can install the magnetic unit separately in front of your existing water separator-fuel filter and it will do the same job while the engine is running, cleaning the fuel as it heads for your engine. The smallest DeBug system will handle a fuel flow of 30 gallons per hour. The complete system costs from $500 to $700. The magnetic unit by itself costs about $150.

A somewhat different approach to the same problem is the PuraTec Fuel Purification System. This system relies upon a small magnetic unit to break up the microbes and a centrifugal unit to remove water, dirt, and microbes from the fuel. It too includes a circulating pump, a

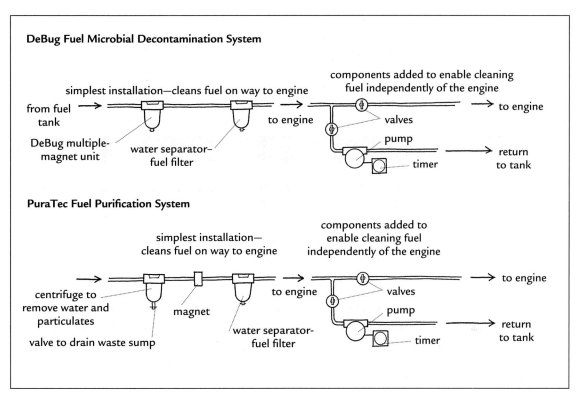

DeBug Fuel Microbial Decontamination System

simplest installation—cleans fuel on way to engine

components added to enable cleaning fuel independently of the engine

from fuel tank

DeBug multiple-magnet unit

water separator–fuel filter

to engine

valves

pump

timer

to engine

return to tank

PuraTec Fuel Purification System

simplest installation—cleans fuel on way to engine

components added to enable cleaning fuel independently of the engine

centrifuge to remove water and particulates

valve to drain waste sump

magnet

water separator-fuel filter

to engine

valves

pump

timer

to engine

return to tank

Two approaches to clean fuel

combined water separator and fuel filter, and a timer and is intended to clean all of the fuel in your tank or to operate while your engine is running. The centrifugal unit intended for sailboat use includes a sump with a 4-ounce capacity to collect contaminants removed from the fuel. The sump must be emptied periodically. The 25-gallon-per-hour unit intended for motorboat use has an 8-ounce-capacity sump and may be preferable. The cost of a 25-gallon-per-hour unit is about $750. An $85 option well worth considering if you go this route is an alarm to alert you when the sump in the centrifugal unit needs emptying.

HEADSAILS

If your boat has two headsails—a jib on the headstay and a staysail on an inner forestay—odds are that you've got a roller-furling genoa on the headstay but a conventionally hanked jib on the inner forestay. The odds are equally good that if your boat is rigged this way, you don't often use the staysail. It's just too much work to unbag it, get it up, take it down, and put it in the bag again. There is, however, an alternative that will likely have you using your staysail just as handily as you use your genoa.

FURLING STAYSAIL

If you convert your staysail to a roller-furling sail, you will find that you use that sail much more often. You can also add to your sailing pleasure by making your staysail tack itself. That way, you'll only need to trim the staysail to suit the point of sail.

To make the staysail self-tending, there are two ways to go—a club boom or a loose foot. The advantage of the club boom is that it gives you better control over the sail's shape without a traveler. The disadvantages are the added weight of the boom assembly on the foredeck and the fact that the club boom itself can be a nuisance. The advantage of the loose-footed staysail is that you don't have the club boom assembly to deal with. The downside is that the loose-footed sail must be cut lower and may interfere with your ability to see forward. It will also be smaller than a boomed staysail and, of course, requires a traveler for the sail to set well.

REMOVABLE INNER FORESTAYS

The problem with removable inner forestays is always what to do with them when you decide to pull them aside. Two solutions seem easily adaptable to a variety of boats.

QUICK-RELEASE SYSTEM

Stowing the inner forestay with quick release

When the stay is disconnected at deck level for stowage off to the side, the quick-release fitting is secured to a shackle or padeye for-

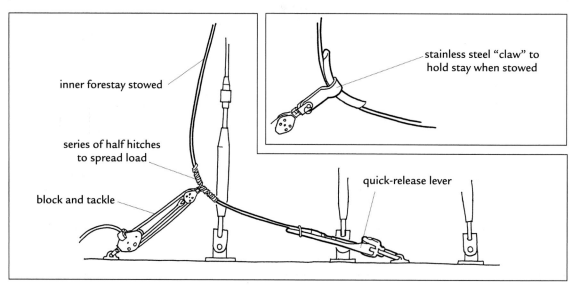

inner forestay stowed

stainless steel "claw" to hold stay when stowed

series of half hitches to spread load

block and tackle

quick-release lever

ward of the aft lower shroud. A small tackle secured to a padeye or shackle near the forward lower shroud chainplate tensions the stay to hold it away from spreaders and shrouds. The tackle can be attached to the stay using multiple wraps of a line or a small stainless "claw" curved to hold the stay under tension without kinking it.

TURNBUCKLE SYSTEM

In place of a quick-release lever, a turnbuckle can be used to tension the stay. From the deck, a turnbuckle is attached to the inner-forestay chainplate using a toggle jaw. At the upper end of the turnbuckle is a short length of rigging wire fitted with a Sta-Lok (or Norseman) eye terminal. At the lower end of the stay is a fork terminal for making the connection to the eye terminal of the turnbuckle assembly. When removed for storage, the jaw fitting on the lower end of the stay can be secured to an eye or other bracket a few inches forward of a forward lower shroud. The length of the turnbuckle assembly will be determined by the need to make the stay itself just long enough to reach its deck fitting near the shroud. When removed for storage, the stay can be secured to the shroud with shock cord. The turnbuckle assembly should be removed and stowed in the cockpit where it will be readily available when needed.

Stowing the inner forestay with turnbuckle release

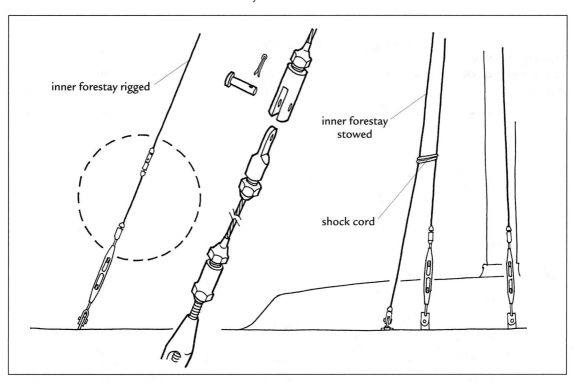

inner forestay rigged

inner forestay stowed

shock cord

LIFTING

One of the more difficult cruising chores is lifting heavy items from the dinghy to the deck—especially the dinghy's outboard motor. Several miniature "cranes" are available to take the sweat out of hoisting heavy equipment, stores, or motors from the dinghy. The best are easily removable (see Seakindliness in chapter 2). In any case, installing a crane is relatively simple.

As an alternative, you may be able to rig a hoist from your boom. While cruising on *Sea Sparrow*, for example, we rigged a four-part block and tackle from the bails for the mainsheet at the boom end to lift our outboard motor from the dinghy into the cockpit. From there it was easy to lift the motor onto the stern-rail motor mount. If you have mid-boom sheeting, you can add a bail near the end of your boom or hang the block and tackle from a strap around the boom. Forged stainless steel bails (made by Schaeffer Marine and Ronstan) are available in a variety of sizes. Note: You *must* use a stainless steel or sturdy aluminum tube as a compression post in your boom when installing a bail.

MAINSAILS

The simplest and most effective way to make handling your mainsail easier is to change from a traditional mainsail to a furling main. There are two approaches to choose between: one in which the mainsail furls vertically either inside or just behind the mast and one in which the mainsail is rolled up inside the boom. Both approaches work well, though there are significant differences between them. Both enable you to raise and lower the sail from the cockpit, and both offer infinite reefing capability. You may lose some light air performance with the mast-furling system because of the reduced sail area. At least one manufacturer of a boom-furling system, on the other hand, claims improved performance because the mainsail is set far enough behind the mast to improve the sail's efficiency (less turbulence from the mast). There are also, of course, differences between brands. For anyone interested, *Practical Sailor* has tested and evaluated the major brands of both mast- and boom-furling systems.

IN-THE-MAST AND BEHIND-THE-MAST FURLERS

In the case of the vertically furling mainsail, the major trade-off is a loss in performance because an in-the-mast or behind-the-mast furl-

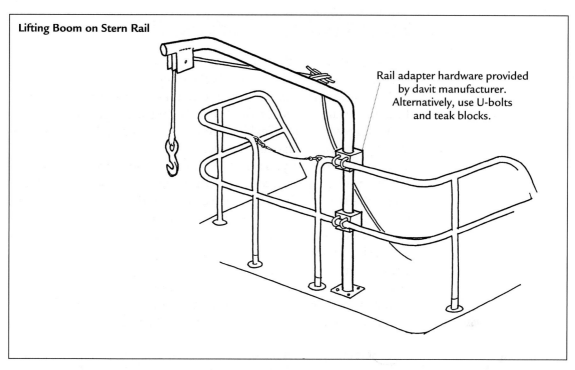

Lifting Boom on Stern Rail

Rail adapter hardware provided by davit manufacturer. Alternatively, use U-bolts and teak blocks.

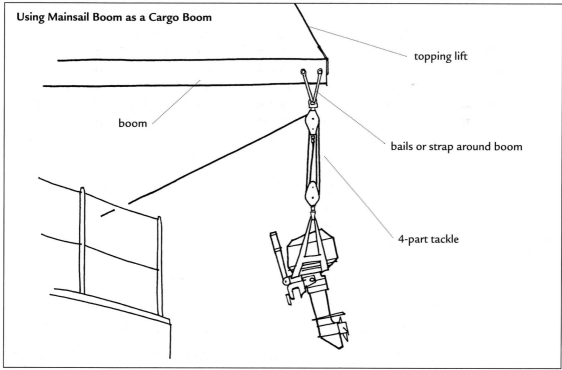

Using Mainsail Boom as a Cargo Boom

topping lift

boom

bails or strap around boom

4-part tackle

Cargo hoists—two approaches

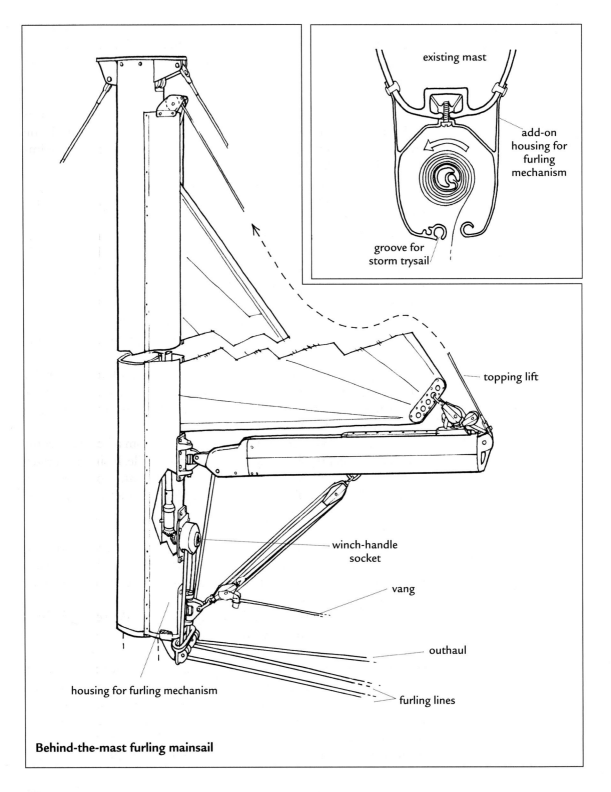

existing mast

add-on housing for furling mechanism

groove for storm trysail

topping lift

winch-handle socket

vang

outhaul

housing for furling mechanism

furling lines

Behind-the-mast furling mainsail

ing mainsail will be about 15 percent smaller than a traditional mainsail with battens and up to 25 percent smaller than a maximum-roach, fully battened main. That means you simply won't sail as fast in light winds.

A vertical furling system for your mainsail also adds 100 to 150 pounds to the mast. While this will tend to increase your boat's roll stability, it may also make your boat heel more easily (though the smaller sail area probably will largely offset that effect). More importantly, the added weight aloft may also affect your boat's righting moment, that is, its ability to upright itself after being knocked down or rolled. Whoever sells and installs a mainsail-furling system should be able to inform you about the impact, if any, of the added weight aloft on your boat's righting moment. If you will be sailing only in protected or semiprotected inland or coastal waters where you will not encounter the large seas usually associated with rolling boats more than 90 degrees, this probably will not be of concern to you. If, however, you have any doubts on the matter, consult the builder or designer of your boat. You might also refer back to the comments under Seakindliness in chapter 2 regarding adding weight aloft to increase roll resistance.

Finally, if something in the system fails, it's a lot harder to make repairs while at sea than it is with a conventional system. So you need some backup—some way of raising a backup mainsail or storm trysail—if you plan to make a long-distance passage.

But—and this is a big "but"—what you gain from all of these compromises is a mainsail that is much easier to handle. It simply doesn't require as much muscle or agility to sail your boat. Moreover, your mainsail is almost infinitely reefable. As the wind picks up, you simply keep rolling in more sail.

When you decide to take this step, you must either purchase an in-the-mast system, in which case you will have to junk your existing mast and start anew; or install a behind-the-mast furling mainsail using your existing mast and rigging. I find the second choice more appealing.

Early behind-the-mast furlers looked much like roller-furling headsail mechanisms rigged behind the mast and adapted to a mainsail. In fact, that's essentially what they were. Today, however, systems are available in which the furling mechanism and the furled sail are shielded within a protective housing that is added to the afterside of the mast. The housing may also include a groove for hoisting a storm trysail, a spare mainsail, or, in an emergency, a headsail fitted with a luff tape. Additionally, the furling mechanisms have been engineered specifically to meet the requirements of a furling mainsail. Your local rigger will be familiar with the behind-the-mast systems available.

One system that comes well recommended is made by Sweden's Selden Mast company and is sold under the brand name Furlex. The list price of the Furlex system ranges from about $3,600 to $8,000 for masts 28 to 57 feet above the deck and booms 12 to 17 feet long. In addition, there is the added cost of a new mainsail. You can have the old mainsail recut as a backup using the luff groove in the Furlex housing.

IN-THE-BOOM FURLING MAINSAILS

In-the-boom furlers are a modern adaptation of the old roller-reefing systems of years past. In those systems you could reef the mainsail by rotating the entire boom so that the sail was shortened by wrapping it around the boom. While these systems were great in principle, they had one major drawback: someone had to stand at the after end of the boom and keep pulling the leech aft as the boom rotated so that the sail would retain its shape. Otherwise the leech tended to walk forward as the boom turned, and the sail bagged horribly. And that is the major problem that developers of in-the-boom furling systems have had to overcome. It is also the problem that makes in-the-boom furling systems a somewhat different animal. That is, although these systems offer infinite reefing and the ability to raise and lower (furl and unfurl) the mainsail from the security of your cockpit, you have to learn some new habits. It may also require a bit more work (effort) to raise, reef, and lower the sail than you expect because of friction inherent in the system.

To overcome the problem of the leech's walking forward, the new boom-furling mainsails are designed with full-length battens. These are not sail-shaping battens; that is, they are not put under tension and used to shape your sail as in modern "full-battened mainsails" (see Above the Waterline in chapter 5). Their primary purpose is to keep the leech of the sail where it's supposed to be as you wind up your sail. To keep the entire foot of the sail from walking forward as you roll it up, the system incorporates a rigid boom vang to hold the boom at the correct angle (parallel to the battens) for rolling up the sail. And you must learn to use that vang for reefing and furling the sail. The topping lift is used mainly to support the boom when the sail is completely furled.

You may also need to luff the sail to furl it, or boom vang or no boom vang, the driving force on the sail will tend to push it forward and may make the sail jam the system as it rolls up. Finally, I mentioned friction inherent in the system. A major difference be-

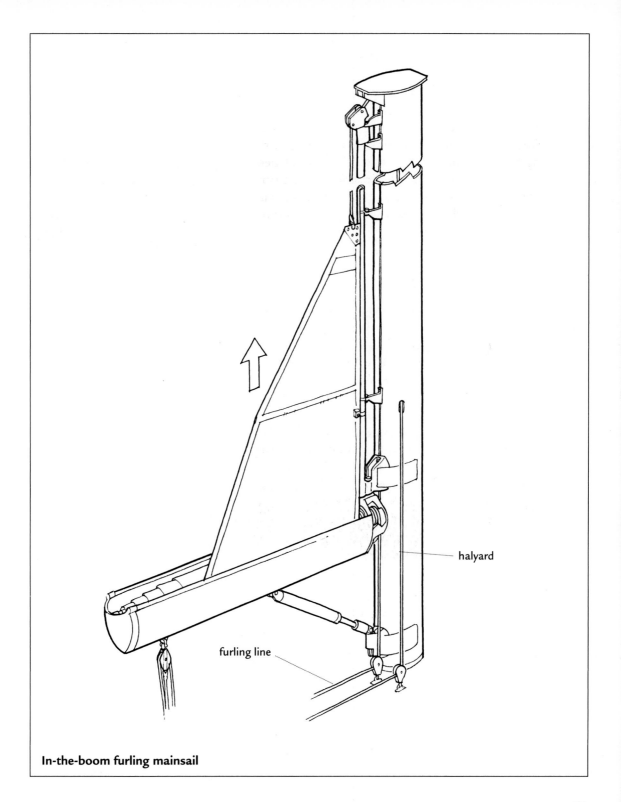

halyard

furling line

In-the-boom furling mainsail

tween the vertically furling mainsail and an in-the-boom system is that you must still raise and lower the mainsail with an in-the-boom furler. In place of slides, the luff of the mainsail is made using a luff tape or modified bolt rope system similar to that used on roller-furling headsails. As the sail is raised, the luff is fed into a grooved mast track. As it is furled (lowered or reefed), the luff comes out of the groove. The friction is inherent in the luff's sliding into the mast track and in the system of turning blocks used to lead the furling lines to the cockpit.

I'm familiar with two in-the-boom furling systems (there are one or two others)—Leisure Furl and ProFurl—both well recommended. The cost of a boom furler for a typical 36-foot cruiser is from $6,000 to $9,000, depending upon the system chosen. Add that to the cost of a new sail.

PILOTING

I will never forget sailing in the Chesapeake Bay one June day in fog and hearing the skippers of two boats querying each other about their location. Each told the other that his loran was not working, and neither one knew where he was. It was particularly memorable because even though we didn't have either a loran or a global positioning system (GPS) at the time and were sailing in the same fog, we had a good idea where we were because we'd been running a dead-reckoning plot.

It's too easy in this age of electronics to neglect paper charts. Moreover, on few boats is it easy for a shorthanded crew to take care of chart work and handle the boat at the same time. Something as simple as a place to display a chart in the cockpit can be a big help.

COCKPIT CHART TABLE

On some boats there is enough space to one side or the other of the companionway sliding hatch to provide a small chart table. A piece of ¼-inch Lucite or Lexan cut to fit the top of the cabinhouse between the sliding hatch and the dodger base provides a good protector and hold-down for the chart when it is in use. You can even use a piano hinge along the companionway edge of the plastic cover to make changing or turning a chart easy.

As an alternative, you can use the top of your sliding hatch in the same way. If there is a ⅜-inch or larger space between the top of the sliding hatch and the edge of the hatch's turtle cover, you can use a Lucite or Lexan cover over your folded chart here as well, though

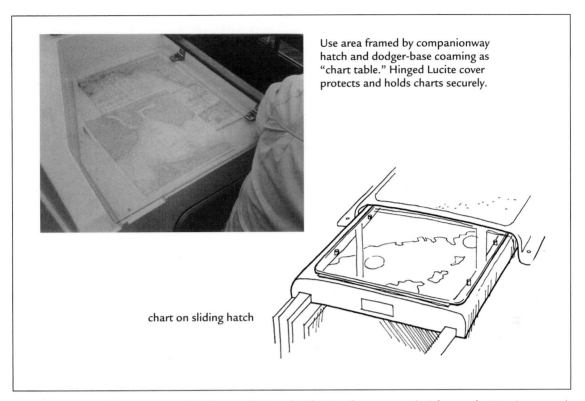

Use area framed by companionway hatch and dodger-base coaming as "chart table." Hinged Lucite cover protects and holds charts securely.

chart on sliding hatch

Cockpit chart tables

probably not hinged. This is the system (without the Lucite cover) that we've used on *Sea Sparrow* for nearly 20 years, using one of the plastic covers sold with BBA Chart Kits to protect our charts in wet weather.

SAIL HANDLING

For family or shorthanded cruising, the more work you can take out of sail handling, the more the crew can enjoy the sailing.

LAZY JACKS

Lazy jacks are such a good idea that it's surprising that more sailors don't have them. Not only do they catch the sail when you drop your mainsail, but if you have four legs to your lazy jacks, you probably won't have to tie in your reef when you need to shorten sail. (Without the four-legged lazy jacks or tying in the reef, the flap of sail that hangs out from the boom when you shorten sail may start fluttering in a strengthening wind, potentially damaging the sail.)

The keys to a good set of lazy jacks are keeping them as simple as possible, having enough vertical lines to contain the sail, and having

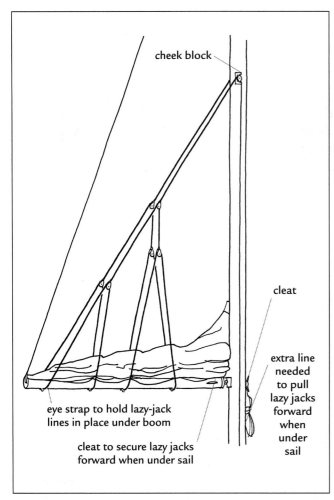

cheek block

cleat

eye strap to hold lazy-jack
lines in place under boom

cleat to secure lazy jacks
forward when under sail

extra line
needed
to pull
lazy jacks
forward
when
under
sail

Lazy jacks

the capability of pulling the rig forward along the boom to stow it out of the way while sailing. You can make your own lazy jacks or you can buy one of several kits available at marine chandleries. Most sailmakers sell kits of their own design. There is also the patented E-Z-JAX system of lazy jacks, which you can have made specifically for your boat. The cost for a set of lazy jacks will be roughly the same no matter whose kit you buy. Figure on from $150 to just over $300, depending upon the length of your boom, and from two to four hours for the installation. Someone will need to climb partway up the mast to install them.

MAINSAIL COVER

The most difficult part of putting on the mainsail cover for those of us who are less than 6 feet tall is being able to reach high enough to secure the cover around the sail piled up at the mast. One solution to that problem is installing mast steps 12 to 18 inches above the deck so that shorter members of the crew will have a footstool to help them get the sail cover in place and secured. Cast-aluminum folding steps can be stowed out of the way when not in use.

MAINSAIL COVER–LAZY JACKS

Not only is it difficult for shorter crew members to secure the mainsail cover at the mast, but the traditional mainsail cover itself can be a bit of a pain. When you take it off, you've got to stow it in a locker somewhere. When you're finished sailing for the day, you need to dig it out of the locker, spread it out on the boom, and keep the wind from blowing it off the sail while you attempt to secure it. I found an alternative—the Mack Pack.

The Mack Pack combines lazy jacks and a sail cover so that the sail cover never leaves the boom. When you want to put up your mainsail, you unzip the sail cover, tuck the two sides out of the way along the boom, and pull the lazy jacks forward. The sail cover is contained by the lazy jacks, which actually run through grommets in the cover. When you take the mainsail down, the lazy jacks and the sail cover capture the sail. You simply tuck the sail away and zip the cover closed. The full cost of the Mack Pack–lazy jack mainsail cover system is about the same as buying lazy jacks and a traditional sail cover separately—about $500. Other sailmakers offer similar products whose cost should be competitive.

Folding steps for use with traditional sail cover and lazy jacks–sail cover combination

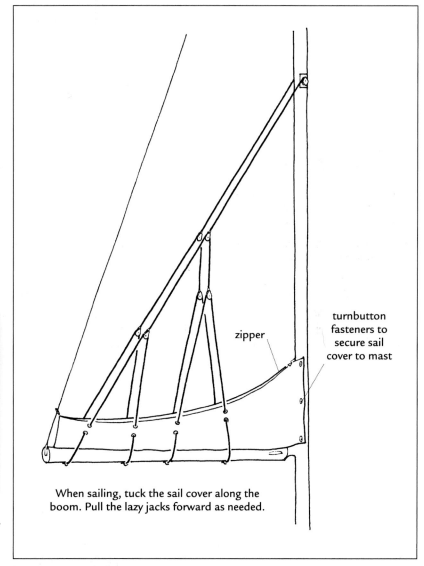

folding step for reaching to put on sail cover

zipper

turnbutton fasteners to secure sail cover to mast

When sailing, tuck the sail cover along the boom. Pull the lazy jacks forward as needed.

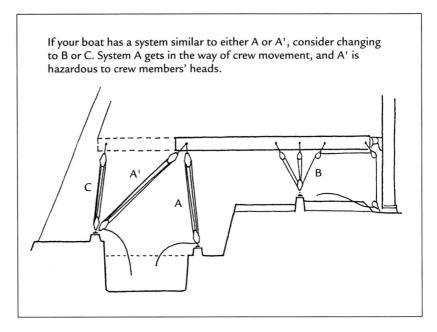

If your boat has a system similar to either A or A', consider changing to B or C. System A gets in the way of crew movement, and A' is hazardous to crew members' heads.

MAINSHEET TRAVELER

On too many aft-cockpit sailboats with short booms the mainsheet traveler is plainly in the way. It is mounted either on the bridge deck, where it is in the way of anyone near the companionway hatch; on a bridge spanning the cockpit between the port and starboard cockpit seats so that you always have to step over it, potentially a serious hazard in rough seas; or on the coaming at the back of the cockpit, so that the mainsheet tries to clip the helmsman's head every time the boom comes across the cockpit.

The problem of misplaced travelers is summed up in two words: short booms. Back in the old days (before the IOR), when booms were just barely short enough to clear the backstay, the mainsheet traveler was routinely mounted effectively and safely on the afterdeck or the coaming at the after end of the cockpit. And the system worked well. But then came the introduction of short booms, which either made the mainsheet's lead hazardous to the helmsman or necessitated moving the traveler forward.

Depending upon the boat, solving the traveler problem may be as simple as getting a boom long enough that a traveler at the back of the cockpit will work well. If a longer boom isn't practical, the only other alternative is to put the traveler on the cabinhouse, bridging the turtle cover for the sliding companionway hatch. You may also need to modify the boom to accommodate the new location of your traveler. The best bet is to consult with a rigger. But one thing's for sure: If the traveler on your boat has been getting in your way and you move it to a more satisfactory location, you'll wonder why you didn't make that change long ago.

MAINSHEET TRAVELER FOR A SMALL CRUISER

One of the cleverer arrangements for a mainsheet traveler on a small cruiser gets the mainsheet and the traveler out of the cockpit by rigging a traveler car that rides on the top of the stern rail. The sturdy stern rail is through-bolted to the deck using ¼- or ⁵⁄₁₆-inch hex head bolts and sturdy backing plates under the deck. This can work on a 24- or 25-foot boat because the mainsail is small. As an added precaution, however, use a preventer routinely or install a "boom brake" to protect the rail from accidental jibes (see Protecting Rig and Propeller in chapter 4).

Stern rail traveler

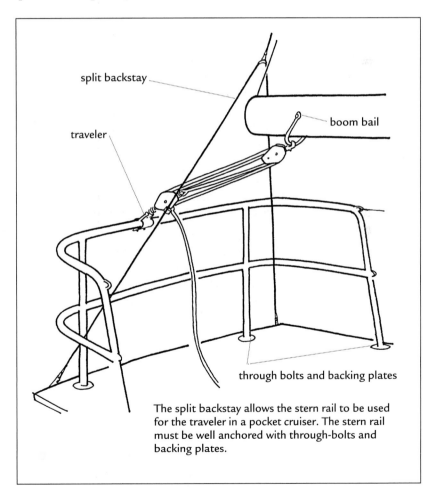

The split backstay allows the stern rail to be used for the traveler in a pocket cruiser. The stern rail must be well anchored with through-bolts and backing plates.

REEFING

If your halyards lead to the cockpit, you may want to install a continuous-line slab-reefing system that also can be operated from the cockpit. With this system in place, you take a reef simply by easing the halyard to a premarked position and pulling the continuous reef line in to its premarked position. Before using your continuous-line reefing system under adverse conditions, however, do one or more test runs at the dock or at anchor to be sure you have marked the halyard and reef line correctly and clearly so that you will not overtighten them and break something when struggling to reef your sail on some dark and stormy night.

Continuous-line slab reefing

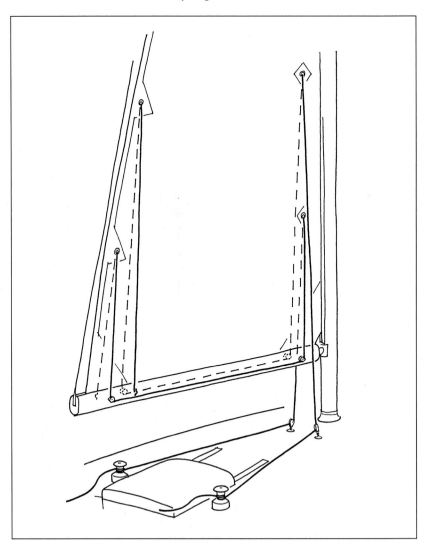

REACHING (WHISKER) POLE

For shorthanded cruising I strongly suggest mounting your reaching pole on a genoa track installed on the front of your mast. I prefer a ball-bearing track and car, which allows you to adjust the car height under load, making it much easier to set and collapse the sail. To move the mast car up and down, use a continuous line through blocks at the top and bottom of the track. You will need to be able to cleat the line to hold the car in place. On larger boats, an Andersen Line Tender will make moving the car much easier. The Line Tender, similar to the self-tailing portion of a self-tailing winch, can be mounted on a short section of track, which makes it easy to tension the continuous line used to move the pole car on the track. All you need then is a winch handle. The Line Tender is distributed in the United States by Scandvik, Inc. The suggested retail price is just under $700.

Stowing the whisker pole on the mast

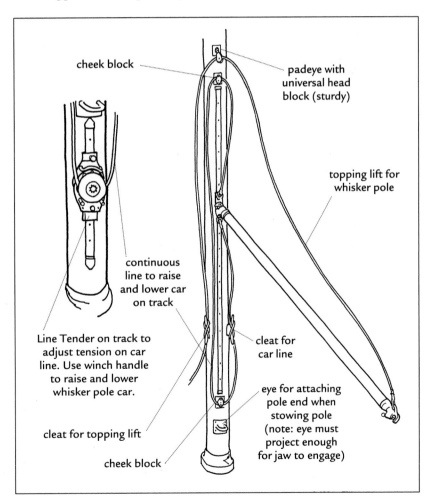

cheek block

padeye with universal head block (sturdy)

topping lift for whisker pole

continuous line to raise and lower car on track

Line Tender on track to adjust tension on car line. Use winch handle to raise and lower whisker pole car.

cleat for car line

cleat for topping lift

eye for attaching pole end when stowing pole (note: eye must project enough for jaw to engage)

cheek block

You can secure the business (sail) end of your pole for stowage to a fitting near the bottom of the mast or on the foredeck near the stemhead. Obviously, if the pole is stowed on the mast, the track must be long enough to accommodate the full pole length. If it is stowed like a fence rail between the mast and the foredeck, the track can be much shorter, but the pole does block your foredeck. In both cases the pole is always ready for use and can be handled easily by one person. If you have sufficient vertical space on your mast, a fixed-length pole is only a fraction of the cost of a telescoping pole, and one length will work with any headsail. The cost of a mast-mounted reaching-pole system is about $1,000.

Note: You may have to remove the jaw at the sail end of your pole and rotate the fitting 180 degrees. The jaw should open facing up so that the jib sheet will lift out cleanly when you open the release. At the mast end, the jaw must open downward. Most poles are sold with both jaws opening in the same direction.

STEERING

Steering is fun when you're out for a lazy day sail. Moreover, there may be times while you're sailing in congested waters, following a channel, or piloting your way from buoy to buoy in a crosscurrent when the close attention you must pay to your course and your surroundings provides challenge and pleasure even to a long stint at the helm. There are times, however, even under these conditions when the skipper must leave the helm for a few moments and there is no one available to take over. If you've got wheel steering, you can just set the wheel lock and do whatever it is that needs doing. The wheel—and therefore the rudder—won't move, and the boat will stay more or less on course.

But what if you have a tiller? And what about the times when you're sailing in open water and steering the same course for several hours, possibly under a hot sun or in a cold rain or overnight? We found pretty quickly on our first 36-hour sail down the East Coast from Delaware Bay to the mouth of the Chesapeake Bay that hand steering under these kinds of circumstances can get old. Fortunately, there are alternatives. And we settled on one before heading from the Chesapeake Bay up to New England the next summer.

AUTOPILOTS

I do not suggest installing an autopilot if most of your sailing is in waters where you've got to follow channels or be alert to dodge other boat traffic. But for open-water sailing when you'll be holding one course for a long time or for motoring on one long course in light air an autopilot can make your day much less tiring. For sailing or motoring in coastal or inshore waters a cockpit autopilot will fill the bill nicely. If, however, you'll be doing much sailing or motoring in a seaway and want to use an autopilot, give serious consideration to a below-deck unit with a hydraulic drive acting directly on an arm or quadrant attached to your rudder post. These hydraulic-drive units are far more powerful and durable than cockpit models that work on your tiller or pedestal wheel steering. For example, although we use *Sea Sparrow*'s tiller-mount cockpit autopilot mainly for motoring offshore when there is no wind, we learned the hard way to carry a spare motor for the autopilot. It simply isn't designed for long use on the constantly rolling ocean even in calm seas.

In choosing a below-deck autopilot the most important thing is to select one that has a history of use on the ocean in all kinds of weather and is powerful enough for your boat. This is not something to pinch pennies on. There has been a consolidation in the industry in recent years, with Simrad buying the Robertson and Navico brands. Autohelm, Nexus, and Raytheon also offer below-deck units. Of the brands listed here, the one I have most often heard favorable comments about from cruisers who have made long ocean passages is the Robertson, now called the Simrad Robertson.

A below-deck autopilot will probably cost in the range of $2,500 to $5,000, depending upon the size (power) of the unit. Installation will cost an additional $1,000 or more. For the record, installing a below-deck autopilot is not a do-it-yourself project. Get someone who knows what he or she is doing to do the job for you.

TILLER LOCK

If you let go of your tiller to tend to your sails or satisfy some other need, chances are that your boat will begin to round up into the wind. If you're motoring, who knows where the boat will start heading. But sometimes, particularly if you're shorthanded, you need to leave the tiller and would like your boat to keep sailing or motoring on more or less the same heading for a minute or two. We've tried lashing the tiller using lines looped over sheet winches or secured to the staysail sheet cleats on the coaming, but neither of these efforts has been satisfactory. It takes too long to get the lashings rigged and unrigged. We've also looked at devices sold for this purpose, but they all involve putting hardware on the tiller.

There is, however, a simple solution to this problem that lets us keep our tiller clear of clutter. All you need is small, flat jam cleats

Tiller lock

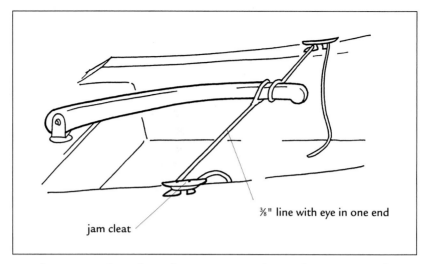

¾" line with eye in one end

jam cleat

on the port and starboard coamings and two short pieces of line, each with an eye in one end. When under sail we just slip the eye of one of those lines over the tiller and secure the other end with a half-turn around the windward jam cleat. When motoring, we run a lashing to each side. We call this system our "tiller lock."

WIND VANES

The wind vane is of little use in protected waters because it steers the boat relative to the wind, not the compass. As a result, the boat tends to wander a bit from your intended track. Although this is not a problem on the open ocean, it is potentially dangerous in waters where maintaining a specific course or avoiding other boat traffic is important.

For sailing on the open ocean or other large bodies of water, however, a good wind vane is worth several additional crew members. In fact, we consider "Homer," *Sea Sparrow*'s Monitor wind vane, almost the most important member of our crew. On any given passage Homer steers the boat 95 percent or more of the time we're under sail and does an excellent job of it, handling most winds and points of sail with equal facility. He's also adept at handling sudden changes in wind strength. Moreover, Homer never complains and doesn't need electricity, diesel fuel, food, or sleep to do his job. And only rarely does he get sick. But if he does, we've got a full complement of spare parts to cure potential ailments. In fact, about his only weakness is steering the boat downwind in light air. But that's when we bring out our tiller-mount autopilot (with its spare motor).

There are several basic types of wind vane, but the principal three are servo-pendulum, pendulum trim tab to main rudder, and pendulum trim tab to auxiliary rudder. All, however, use the flow of air (wind) over an air vane (consider it a wing that sticks up in the air) to steer the boat. As the wind shifts or the boat changes direction relative to the wind, the air flowing over the vane pushes it to one side or the other. That motion from side to side is converted by a system of gears into a twisting force that is used either directly or indirectly to steer the boat.

Servo-pendulum. In a servo-pendulum wind vane the twisting force generated from the air vane is applied to a paddle projecting down in the water. That paddle, in turn, is connected by two lines leading through a series of blocks to the boat's tiller or wheel steering. When there is no need for course correction, the water flows evenly down both sides of the paddle and the paddle hangs in line with the boat's keel. If the air vane is pushed to one side or the other by a change in

Servo-pendulum wind vanes—two different design approaches

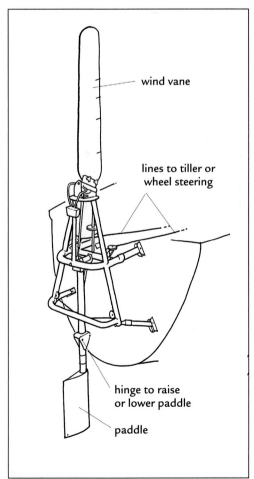

wind vane

lines to tiller or wheel steering

hinge to raise or lower paddle

paddle

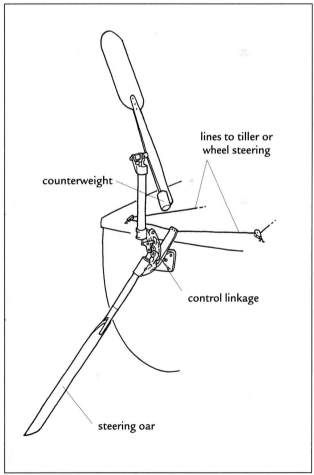

lines to tiller or wheel steering

counterweight

control linkage

steering oar

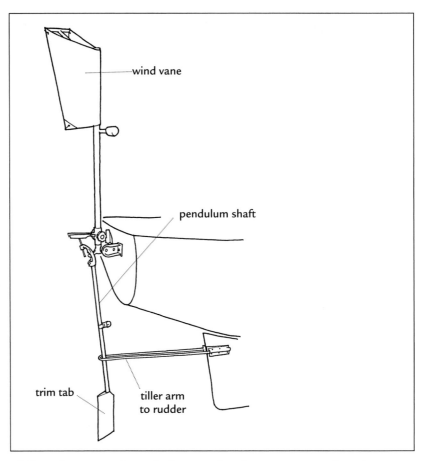

wind vane

pendulum shaft

trim tab

tiller arm
to rudder

airflow, however, the twisting motion it generates makes the water paddle turn so that the water pushes against one side or the other of the paddle, moving it sideways. This movement of the paddle from side to side pulls on first one steering line and then the other, twitching the tiller or wheel back and forth to adjust the course being steered. It sounds (and looks) like a Rube Goldberg device, but it works well. Moreover, the faster the boat goes through the water, the more water pressure is forced against the paddle and the stronger the pull is on the steering lines. The result is a primary advantage of the servo-pendulum wind vane—its ability to steer the boat even in severe conditions.

Pendulum trim tab to main rudder. In a pendulum-trim-tab-to-main-rudder wind vane the water paddle is used to control the rudder directly without going through the tiller or wheel steering. The water paddle passes through a sturdy, usually long U-shaped bracket that extends aft from the rudder and in effect becomes a trim tab. As the movement of the wind vane twists the water paddle, making it move

Trim-tab-to-auxiliary-rudder wind vane

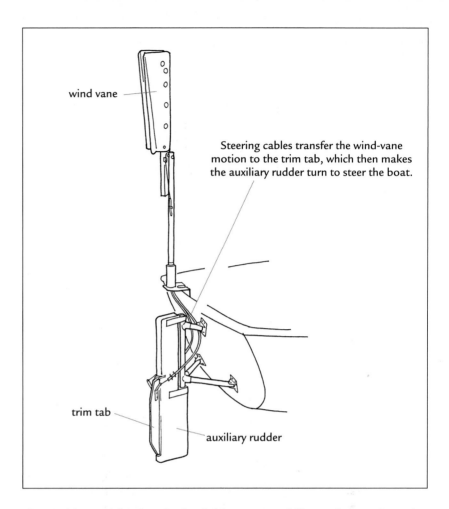

wind vane

Steering cables transfer the wind-vane motion to the trim tab, which then makes the auxiliary rudder turn to steer the boat.

trim tab

auxiliary rudder

from side to side, the shaft of the water paddle pushes against the U-bracket, moving the rudder to one side or the other. This is the patented Sayes Rig. It is used with particular advantage on boats with hydraulic steering as well as on large boats.

Trim tab to auxiliary rudder. In a trim-tab-to-auxiliary-rudder wind vane the paddle projecting into the water is an auxiliary rudder held straight up and down in line with the keel. It does not swing from side to side but rotates on its own rudder shaft just as a normal rudder does. A small trim tab mounted on its trailing edge connects to the wind vane. As the air vane is pushed from side to side by the wind, that motion is used to turn the trim tab to one side or the other, and the force of water flowing past the trim tab turns the auxiliary rudder to steer the boat. The boat's own rudder is not used to steer. Instead it is locked in place, set to give the auxiliary rudder an almost neutral helm. This system is particularly effective in light air and often can be used when a boat's configuration makes the use of other wind vanes problematic. It may be less effective, however, in severe weather because of the relatively small size of the auxiliary rudder.

The most up-to-date source of the names, addresses, and telephone numbers of companies selling the several different brands and styles of wind vanes is the self-steering section of the classified ads in major sailing and cruising magazines.

TAKING ON FUEL AND WATER

For the most part, taking on fuel and water is relatively straightforward. Unfortunately, however, mistakes may result in fuel being pumped into a water tank, or water into a fuel tank. Believe it or not, it does happen.

COLOR CODING OR LABELING DECK FILLS

If your boat has water and fuel, waste and fuel, or water and waste fill pipes on the same stretch of deck—I've even seen boats with four water and fuel deck fills lined up neatly right next to one another—consider labeling or color coding the deck fills to protect against someone's inadvertently putting fuel into your water tank or waste tank or water into your fuel tank. Otherwise, you've got an accident waiting to happen.

The best safeguard is to label each fill pipe (e.g., "diesel," "water," etc.) using a two-part polyurethane coating and a stencil. As an alternative, depending upon the brand of your fill pipes, you may be able to purchase color-coded plugs for them. If not, you may be able to color code your bronze or chromed deck pipes using an epoxy or enamel intended specifically for coating metal. Try an art-supply store. Still another alternative is to color code the pipes by painting colored rings around them. Use green for diesel fuel, red for gasoline, blue for water, and brown for waste. Whatever system you use, it will be an improvement.

4 MAKE YOUR BOAT
More Seaworthy

Seaworthiness becomes an issue mainly when you decide to sail out into the ocean or onto other large bodies of water where wind and sea conditions can deteriorate dramatically and there is no place to go for shelter. Your boat has to get you through the storm—with your help, of course. But the fact is that a good, seaworthy boat can often take a lot more punishment than the crew.

Another equally important fact is that many, if not most, of the sailboats sold in the world were not designed for serious offshore sailing. Within practical limits, there is very little you can do to make these boats seaworthy. There is a second group of boats, however, that can be made seaworthy for ocean sailing with some significant modifications. And a smaller, third group of boats were both designed and constructed with long-distance blue-water cruising in mind. Some among this last group can be taken offshore straight from the factory after only a shakedown cruise to make sure that all systems function as intended. Most, however, can benefit from additions that you can make yourself or have made locally without spending an outrageous amount of money.

I start with one basic assumption—that your boat was designed and constructed for coastal or offshore sailing. If you have any doubts about that, you should seek out a qualified marine surveyor and ask whether in his or her judgment your boat is fit for the cruising you intend and what improvements you should make.

Assuming that you already believe your boat is fundamentally suitable for coastal, ocean, or long-distance Great Lakes sailing, you should consider the prime areas for improving its seaworthiness: (1) guarding against collision, (2) keeping the crew safely on the boat, (3) keeping the crew safe when they are down below, (4) keeping the ocean outside of your boat, (5) preparing for foul weather, and (6) protecting your rig or propeller.

GUARDING AGAINST COLLISION

Unfortunately, one of the greatest hazards to cruisers on small boats is collision at sea. It does not happen often, but the results are usually catastrophic when it does. When cruising the oceans with a limited crew (i.e., one or two adults), it simply is not possible to keep an alert watch at all times. Moreover, in heavy winds, seas, rain, or fog even an alert crew has limited visibility, so that a sailboat moving at five or six knots can be hard pressed to get out of the way at the last minute of a ship moving at 20 knots or more. What this means is that you should do whatever you can to make your boat more visible to other vessels and to enhance your ability to keep a lookout.

NAVIGATION LIGHTS

The U.S. Coast Guard requires that the red and green bow lights on recreational boats less than 12 meters long (about 39 feet) be visible from a distance of one mile and that the white steaming light and the white stern light be visible from a distance of two nautical miles. For boats between 12 meters and 20 meters (about 65 feet) the visibility requirements are two nautical miles for the red and green bow lights as well as for the white stern and steaming lights.

Theoretically, your boat's navigation lights satisfy those requirements. Practical reality may differ from theory, however. Although your lights may, in fact, be visible at those distances when atmospheric conditions are perfect, when the sea is dead calm, when the viewer knows where to look and what to look for, and when there are no other lights on or near the water to compete for the viewer's attention, the likelihood is that your boat's running lights will be considerably less visible under more normal sailing conditions. If you add to that reality check the fact that many boat builders install the least expensive navigation lights available to satisfy the Coast Guard's requirements, you may well find this an area ripe for upgrading.

But first check to see how good (or bad) your running lights are by

Upgrading running lights

A bow rail mount for your red-green combination light will be 2–3 feet higher than deck- or hull-mounted lights. To move your red-green lights to the bow rail, remove the rail and fish the wire up through the rail from under the deck. Bed the rail's feet well with a silicone-acrylic caulk. Seal the hole in the rail where the wire emerges with the same caulk. To move a transom-mounted stern light to the stern rail, use a similar approach.

comparing the lights now on your boat to those shown in the equipment catalogs for boats up to 20 meters long. Those lights will have 25-watt bulbs. Also, the red and green bow light or lights will be rated for a visibility of two miles. Yes, they will use more power than smaller lights with 5- or 10-watt bulbs, but your boat will be more visible and you will be safer.

Also check to see whether you can put larger bow or stern lights on your boat. Although larger lights are not necessarily rated for visibility at longer distances, the mere fact that they are larger will make them easier to see. And even if these lights look a bit big for your boat, you may decide that the added margin of safety they offer is worth the aesthetic compromise.

In addition to optimizing the size and power of your running lights, you can make sure that your navigation lights are located where they will have maximum visibility. For starters, higher is better. So, for example, if your stern light is mounted in or on the transom, consider moving it to the stern rail. If you have an equipment arch or pole at the stern, consider moving the light higher still. Just be sure that the light is shielded so that it will not interfere with your night vision when you look astern.

The same dictum—higher is better—applies to red and green bow lights. If they are in the hull, consider moving them to the bow rail. Locating the lights, or a red-and-green combination light, just below and aft of the leading edge of the upper bow rail will afford them some protection from damage and will position them at least 2 feet higher. Finally, consider using a masthead tricolor light when you are under sail at sea (boats under 20 meters). Its height and its 25-watt bulb make it more easily seen from a distance, especially in waters where even normal seas will obscure deck-level lights.

RADAR

The great single advantage of modern radars is that you can draw an electronic circle around your boat and program the radar to sound an alarm if it "sees" another boat within that circle. It's tantamount to having an electronic eye on watch—not a perfect eye, to be sure, but a very good one.

Not long ago radar was a luxury on a cruising sailboat. Today the combination of miniaturization and reduction in cost has almost reached the point (prices range from $1,000 to $3,000) at which radar can become as much an item of standard equipment for the long-distance cruising sailor as a single sideband or ham radio—even on many smaller boats. For example, some systems have antennae weighing as little as 8.8 pounds. The radar units them-

Backstay self-leveling radar mounts

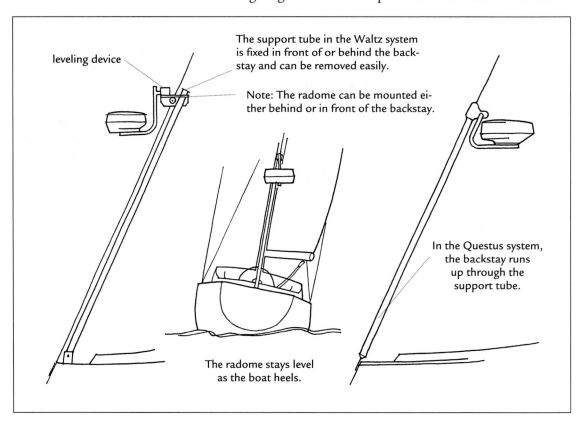

leveling device

The support tube in the Waltz system is fixed in front of or behind the backstay and can be removed easily.

Note: The radome can be mounted either behind or in front of the backstay.

In the Questus system, the backstay runs up through the support tube.

The radome stays level as the boat heels.

selves have become so small that they're not much larger than the GPS or loran unit of a few years ago. Moreover, their displays are readable even in sunlight. Power requirements range from about 2 to 5 amps, but some units offer a "watch standing" feature, which sets the radar to scan the horizon only at set intervals, such as every 5 minutes, so that the actual power consumption may be quite low.

There are also more options now for where to mount the radar antenna. The two I find interesting are pole mounts for the stern and backstay mounts. On larger boats, where the addition of 50 pounds or so for a radar pole and antenna may have little impact on the boat's trim or motion (see Seakindliness in chapter 2), a pole mount is a viable option. Usually the pole will be tied into your stern rail for bracing purposes. The likely cost of a fixed aluminum or stainless steel pole mount ranges from about $200 to more than $700. Options, including a leveling system, can add hundreds more to the cost. A 1999 review of pole-mount radar systems in *Practical Sailor* listed the Garhauer radar pole as a "best buy" but noted that was also the heaviest of those evaluated. The editors also called Nautical Engineering's adjustable pole "an excellent value" and noted that Edson offers the "most complete, high quality, adaptable line" of poles. The best pole, according to *Practical Sailor*, was also the most expensive (about $2,300) and lightest in weight (less than 10 pounds)—a carbon-fiber-composite pole from Forespar. Maybe for the serious racing sailor . . .

Self-leveling (gimbaled) backstay mounts provide an interesting alternative to the stern pole mount, particularly if you want to minimize the impact of the additional weight on the stern. Although the vertical-beam width of most modern radars is sufficient that you do not begin to lose effectiveness until the boat heels more than 15 degrees, a gimbaled radar mount is appealing, particularly for use at sea, when sailing wing and wing downwind routinely results in significant and constant rolling. Of the two gimbaled backstay mounts I've seen—the Questus and the Waltz—*Practical Sailor* gave the "best buy" rating to the Waltz in a 1998 review. The Questus system retails for about $1,000, the Waltz for about $800. Both can be purchased at substantial discount from major marine stores.

RADAR DETECTORS

In the search for an active system for detecting the presence of ships, a modern radar detector offers an alternative—or backup—to radar, particularly on smaller boats where radar is simply impractical or where battery power is at a premium. Radar detectors that I've seen use barely more than 1 amp per day while standing a continuous watch. Even the best radar detector, however, won't tell you a ship's out there unless that ship's radar is turned on.

RADAR REFLECTORS

We had an eye-opening experience near the end of a nine-day passage from Beaufort, North Carolina, to the British Virgin Islands. Winds were easterly at about 25 knots, seas were running 6 to 9 feet, and we were sailing on a beam reach under a double-reefed mainsail and staysail when we were called on the VHF shortly before noon by a U.S. aircraft carrier and asked our course and speed. The carrier was about 2 miles off our starboard quarter on a course that would carry it safely astern, so there was no hazard. After providing the information, however, we asked whether they could see us on their

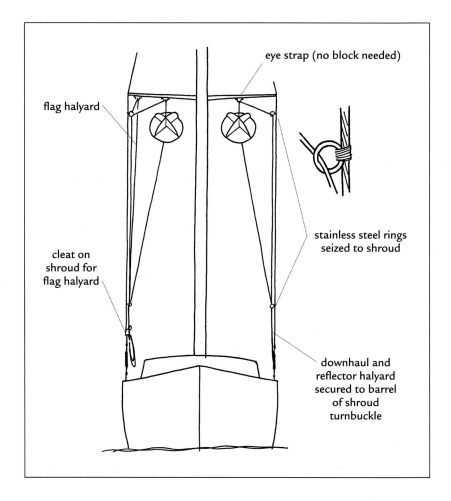

Doubling up on radar reflectors

radar. The answer was "Negative." They had only a visual sighting of us.

That response was sobering. When a U.S. aircraft carrier cannot distinguish a boat from sea clutter on its radar system despite a boat's top-rated radar reflector, it is reasonable to conclude that almost any cruising sailboat may be invisible to large ships' radar at one time or another.

Does that mean that radar reflectors are worthless? Absolutely not. The ocean is not always as rough as it was on the day we spoke with the aircraft carrier. We have subsequently been assured by other vessels that we were visible on their radar in calmer conditions. Our experience does point out, however, the value of having the most effective radar reflector available. It also suggests that there might be value in flying more than one radar reflector to increase the size of your reflected signal. According to experts I've consulted, a second radar reflector should double the size of your reflected signal and in theory, at least, make you more visible to other vessels.

How do you know which radar reflector is the most effective? It's not necessarily the most expensive or the fanciest. In tests conducted for *Practical Sailor* over the years, the standard Davis anodized aluminum Echomaster radar reflector (about $35 at discount and widely available) has consistently outperformed radar reflectors costing several times as much.

KEEPING CREW ON THE BOAT

It doesn't make any difference how well your boat is able to stand up to wind and sea if you and your boat part company. Fortunately, most of the steps you can take to make sure you stay aboard are not by themselves particularly costly. I suggest some improvements— cockpit grab bars, adding a second lifeline, mast rails, and strengthening lifeline stanchions—in chapter 2. For offshore sailing, however, additional improvements are worth considering.

BOW AND STERN RAILS

If your boat does not have double bow and stern rails, that's a weakness worth correcting. This is a job you probably cannot do yourself. It involves bending stainless steel tubes to fairly precise measurements and welding them in place. The only practical way to get the job done is to remove the existing rails and take them to a welding shop to have middle rails added. If you don't have access under the deck to the fasteners securing your rails, do not try to get the welding done in place. The risks and the difficulty are too great to make it worthwhile. According to experts I've consulted, your time would be better spent creating access to the underside of those fittings so that you can remove them. If nothing else, this would enable you to rebed them and probably stop a future leak. It would also, of course, make it possible for you to take them to the shop to have the middle rail added. Cost estimates for this work range from $400 to $700 per rail.

BULWARKS

Bulwarks are usually associated with heavy-displacement, traditional cruisers. They serve a valid purpose, however, and there's no reason why wood bulwarks can't be added to modern fiberglass cruising boats, even those with slotted aluminum toe rails. I first saw this idea described more than 20 years ago in Hal Roth's book *After 50,000 Miles,* where he described adding bulwarks to *Whisper* by bolting 1-by-4-inch teak planks to sturdy Everdur plates welded to his bronze stanchion bases. These teak bulwarks were mounted ¾ inch above the deck after Roth removed *Whisper*'s wood toe rail so that water could run off under them.

On modern boats, where slotted aluminum toe rails are integral structural members, I prefer a variation on Roth's idea, that is, fastening the bulwark to the stanchions themselves so that the bulwark will be right at the top of the stanchion bases. On most boats this would be from ½ to 1 inch above the aluminum toe rail.

The first step is to decide how much of the deck you want enclosed with your bulwarks. On *Sea Sparrow*, for example, we would run the bulwarks from the bow rail aft to the lifeline gates amidship. You may want to run them only from the bow rail to the second stanchion. If you can make each bulwark from one piece of teak, it will follow the curve of your hull naturally as you bend it gently around each stanchion. If you use more than one board for the run, you have two alternatives: joining the boards at a stanchion or running the boards between stanchions rather than outboard of them. The advantage of joining them at a stanchion is that the bulwark will more or less follow the curve of the hull, almost as if it were a single board. If the bulwarks run between stanchions, they will follow the line of your lifelines and lie inside your toe rail. Finally, look at the distance between your stanchions and decide whether to add intermediate supports in the form of peglike stanchions just long enough to reach the top of the bulwark.

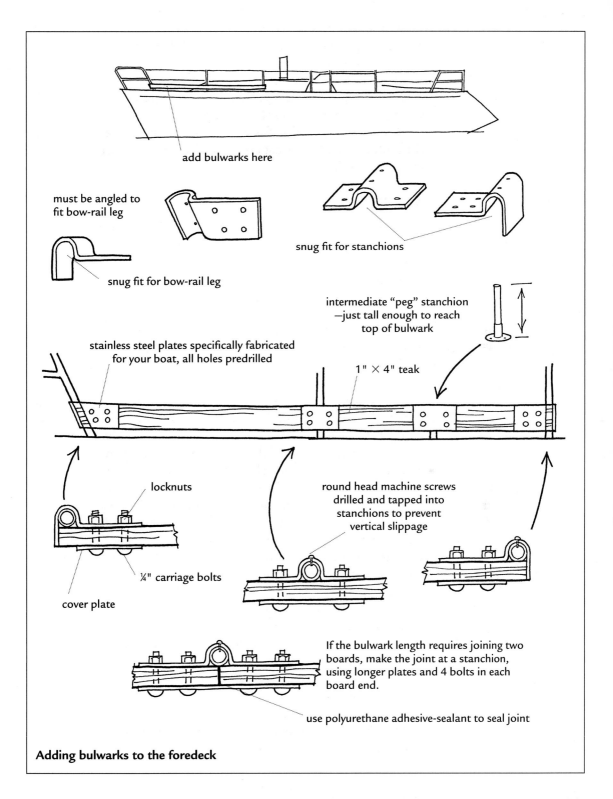

add bulwarks here

must be angled to
fit bow-rail leg

snug fit for stanchions

snug fit for bow-rail leg

intermediate "peg" stanchion
—just tall enough to reach
top of bulwark

stainless steel plates specifically fabricated
for your boat, all holes predrilled

1" × 4" teak

locknuts

round head machine screws
drilled and tapped into
stanchions to prevent
vertical slippage

¼" carriage bolts

cover plate

If the bulwark length requires joining two
boards, make the joint at a stanchion,
using longer plates and 4 bolts in each
board end.

use polyurethane adhesive-sealant to seal joint

Adding bulwarks to the foredeck

As an alternative to Roth's method of adding support plates to your stanchion bases, have a shop that fabricates stainless steel make the cover plates and stanchion-wrap plates (see drawing page 77) needed to mount your bulwarks. The stanchion-wrap plate should fit tightly around the stanchion. The board will be secured by bolting it between the stanchion-wrap plate on the inside and a cover plate on the outside. Use machine screws tapped into the stanchions so that the bulwarks cannot slide up or down on the stanchions.

Fabrication of the stainless steel will probably cost from $300 to $700, depending upon where you live and how many stanchions are involved. Once that work is done, however, installing the bulwarks should be easy. Moreover, they'll be easy to remove should that ever be necessary.

COCKPIT EGRESS

On some boats, staysail or primary jibsheet winches are set on the coaming, close enough to the cabinhouse that the winches and their sheet leads get in the way of the crew's feet when they step out of the cockpit to go forward. We get accustomed to stepping over or around them. In heavy weather offshore, however, those winches can become trippers, which is not good when every step is difficult because of sea conditions. If this describes the sheet winches on your boat, consider the feasibility of moving the winches aft. It may require changing the sheet lead, a bit of teak woodworking to repair the coaming where you've removed the winches, or adding a stainless steel rub strake to protect the edge of the coaming from chafe, but moving the winches as little as a few inches can make a major difference in clearing the pathway out of the cockpit.

COCKPIT HANDHOLDS

Cockpits need things for the crew to hold onto, especially in a seaway. Moreover, the larger the cockpit, the more handholds you need. In plain words, you should never have to let go of one handhold before you have fastened your other hand securely on the next one. The dodger frame offers a good place for grab bars, or handholds (see page 31). The companionway hatch, the bimini frame, and the coaming offer others.

For example, a short handrail across the front of the sliding companionway hatch is conveniently located when the hatch is closed. When the hatch is open, it also can be a reassuring handhold when going down the companionway ladder.

Companionway grab bars

Your bimini frame can also serve as a series of handholds on each side of the cockpit if the frame is made of stainless steel tubing rather than aluminum. In a large cockpit, mini-handrails welded to the underside of the bimini's overhead frame make excellent handholds.

As for the cockpit coaming, if the self-tailing feature of your sheet winches has taken the place of cleats for securing jibsheets, a couple of cleats (with fairly large backing plates) located where they can be used if needed for your jibsheets make excellent handholds when making your way aft or forward in the cockpit. You're bound to find other uses for them as well—for example, as a backup to the winch if you ever need to secure a sheet while it's under load so that you can remove it from the winch without letting the jib fly.

COCKPIT SAFETY-HARNESS ATTACHMENTS

The number of attachment points needed for hooking on the crew's safety harnesses depends upon the size of the cockpit and the number in the crew. On *Sea Sparrow*, the 6-foot lead on our safety harnesses lets us reach all parts of the cockpit from a single stout U-bolt secured with a backing plate immediately below the companionway. We can hook on before coming into the cockpit and stay attached till we are safely below. The U-bolt is also large enough to accept easily both of our safety-harness clips at the same time.

If you have a larger cockpit, you may need a second attachment

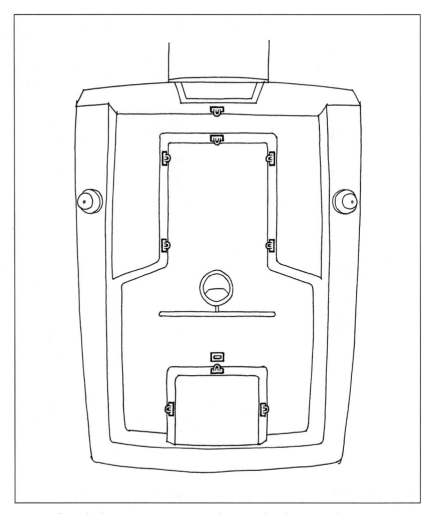

point for a helmsman. You may also need other attachment points
so that, with two leads on your harness, you can clip onto a second
attachment before unclamping from the first as you make your way
through the cockpit. In all cases, however, you should be able to
hook on with your harness before going out into the cockpit and
remain hooked on until you are safely below.

In general, attachments should be low in the cockpit and as close
to the centerline as possible so that your harness's lead can pull you
up short before you go over or through the lifelines if a sea sweeps
the cockpit. U-bolts or heavy-duty padeyes through-bolted to the
side of the footwall at about sole level often will serve well. For the
helmsman, I suggest installing a U-bolt or padeye in the cockpit
sole on the boat's centerline at the base of the helmsman's seat (not
at the base of the steering pedestal) so that he or she can clip on or

off while seated. In any case, it should be positioned so that even the shortest crew member can hook onto it easily when at the helm. Note: Do not use folding padeyes for safety-harness attachments. You should be able to clip on and off easily with one hand, which is not possible if you have to fumble around to lift the eye before you can hook on or off.

COMPANIONWAY HANDRAILS

Sturdy handrails inside and outside the cabinhouse along both sides (port and starboard) of the companionway often are a great addition to a cruising boat. In an active seaway, climbing the companionway ladder and getting through the companionway into the cockpit can be surprisingly difficult. Sturdy handholds inside and out make the job easier and safer. The exterior companionway handholds are also useful even when you are simply sitting in the cockpit. They are something to hold onto, which can be very nice in boisterous conditions.

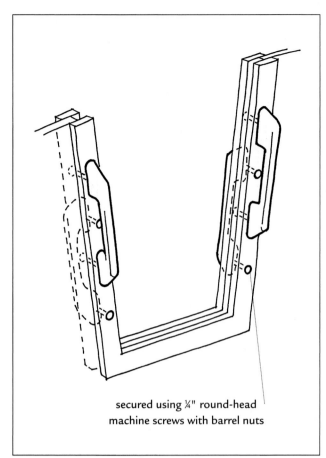

secured using ¼" round-head machine screws with barrel nuts

Companionway handrails

HANDRAILS ON DECK

If you have to go on deck when the wind's blowing 40 knots and the seas are 12 to 14 feet and building, you will need something more than lifelines to hold on to. Your boat should have sturdy handrails along the full length of the cabinhouse. If you have a large, clear foredeck, a sturdy handrail through-bolted down the middle of the deck or a ⅝-inch rope stretched taut between the mast and bow that you can hold on to as you crawl forward (you won't be walking) will be greatly appreciated.

JACK LINES

A jack line is a safety line—of wire, rope, or nylon webbing—that runs the length of your deck both port and starboard. It's there for you to hook your harness to before leaving the cockpit. It should allow you to move all over the boat, with the hook from your harness slid-

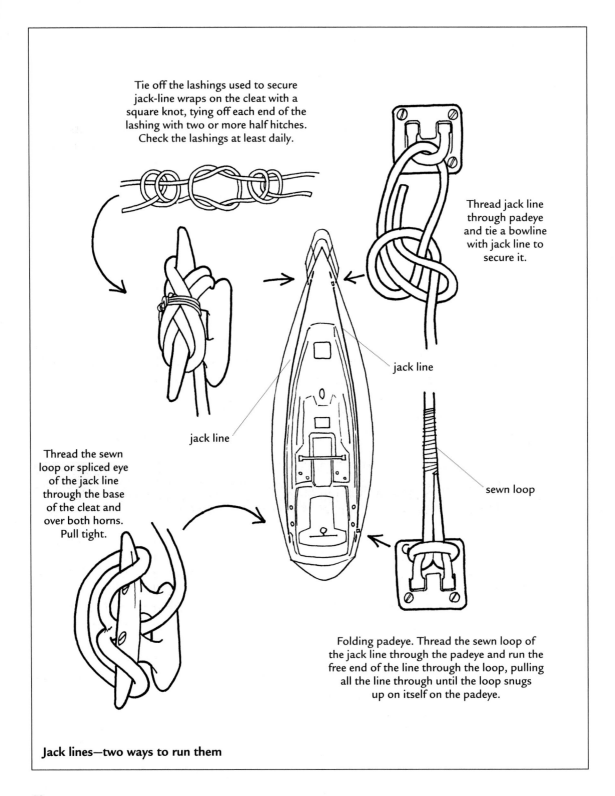

Tie off the lashings used to secure jack-line wraps on the cleat with a square knot, tying off each end of the lashing with two or more half hitches. Check the lashings at least daily.

Thread jack line through padeye and tie a bowline with jack line to secure it.

jack line

jack line

sewn loop

Thread the sewn loop or spliced eye of the jack line through the base of the cleat and over both horns. Pull tight.

Folding padeye. Thread the sewn loop of the jack line through the padeye and run the free end of the line through the loop, pulling all the line through until the loop snugs up on itself on the padeye.

Jack lines—two ways to run them

ing along the jack line as you move about. Some newer boats come equipped with folding padeyes on the foredeck and near the stern for use when rigging your jack lines. The advantage of the folding padeye is that it is out of the way when you don't need it, which, of course, is most of the time. The padeyes must, however, be through-bolted with backing plates and well bedded.

You can also rig jack lines between your bow and stern cleats. I suggest lashing the layers of hitches on the cleats used to secure the jack lines, however, to be certain that they cannot work loose. Nylon webbing, available from almost any sailmaker, has become the jack-line material of choice for many sailors because it does not roll under your foot if you step on it, as rope or wire will do.

LIFELINES

The upper lifeline should be at least 24 but preferably 26 inches above deck level. From an aesthetic viewpoint, 24- or 26-inch lifelines may seem too high on a small boat, but lower lifelines are simply not acceptable for sailing offshore. Also, your stanchions should feel sturdy when you push or lean against them. If they feel soft, or if you can see or feel the deck flexing under the stanchions, you'll need to reinforce the stanchion bases. Finally, if your boat is equipped with only single lifelines, adding a lower wire to both the lifelines and the gates is worthwhile. Those conversions are also illustrated in the Security section beginning on page 30.

KEEPING CREW SAFE BELOW DECK

A surprising number of boats whose external appearance suggests that they are intended for offshore sailing turn out, upon examination of their interiors, to be suitable mostly for use at the dock. For example, the deck may be well equipped with handholds for the crew to use when going forward to work with a sail, but the main cabin may be almost cavernous, with few places to hold on to when trying to move about in a seaway.

"One hand for the boat, one hand for yourself" is an admonition we all give new sailors when they first step aboard. Although the focus of that advice is usually centered on moving about the deck because of the obvious risk of unwary guests falling overboard, that same advice is just as important below deck. When sailing in a seaway or even in calm water with other boat traffic, the crew down below has no way of knowing when the boat will lurch suddenly or be rolled violently, potentially sending someone across the cabin. I know one relatively experienced sailor who suffered two broken ribs and a severe head laceration that way while serving as part of a delivery crew. The boat had nothing you could really grab on to when passing through the cabin.

There is also the matter of cabin lights at night. Generally speaking, no white lights should be used below (or on deck, for that matter) when sailing at night. Not only does the crew on watch need its night vision to be protected from white lights coming up from the cabin but the rest of the crew needs its night vision intact in case they are called to help with a sail change. But it's not enough to protect night vision; the below-deck crew also needs to be able to see! And for that they need lights.

COMPANIONWAY LADDER

You must be able to secure the companionway ladder so that it will stay in place no matter what happens. Usually that means fasteners at top and bottom, most likely hooks, slide bolts, or ladder hooks. However, you can take most of the strains off those fasteners with the strategic use of two short pieces of teak. A few additional even smaller pieces of teak will make your ladder easier to climb when the boat is under sail. Wedges made to fit the outer 4 inches or so on both ends of each step will provide a more nearly horizontal surface near the downhill edge of the step when the boat is heeling.

GRAB BAR IN THE HEAD

Every head should have at least one grab bar—a handhold you can easily reach when the boat lurches (see drawings page 86). Towel bars usually are not strong enough to serve. In addition, if the head geography permits, a handrail at about elbow height next to the toilet—one on each side if possible—will often help you stay on the toilet seat in a seaway. Finally, a piece of teak across the head sole where someone seated can brace him- or herself with a foot against the boat's motion may also be helpful. On *Sea Sparrow*, whose head is small, we have a 2-foot teak handrail positioned at a small angle on the bulkhead so that a person on the toilet can lay his left forearm and hand comfortably along the rail and hold on tight. The head's countertop, with a sturdy 2-inch fiddle, is immediately to the person's right, offering another handhold. The bottom of the door frame provides a foot brace, necessary when the boat is heeled well over. Under more benign conditions the handrail serves for hanging small towels or washcloths.

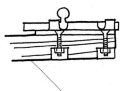

Barrel bolts bolted to teak board using small machine screws before teak is installed at top of ladder. Drill out the back of the teak board to countersink the flat washers and nuts. Fill the cavity with caulk.

1" × 4" teak screwed to cabinhouse and liner

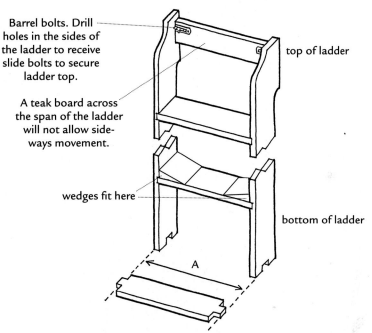

Barrel bolts. Drill holes in the sides of the ladder to receive slide bolts to secure ladder top.

top of ladder

A teak board across the span of the ladder will not allow sideways movement.

wedges fit here

bottom of ladder

A

Using teak the same width as the ladder legs, cut it to match the outside width of the ladder (A). Cut the board ends as shown and notch the bottom of the ladder legs to fit over the tabs on the board ends. Screw the teak board to the cabin sole only after putting the ladder in place so that the board is positioned exactly. Once the top and bottom are secured as illustrated, this ladder will stay put.

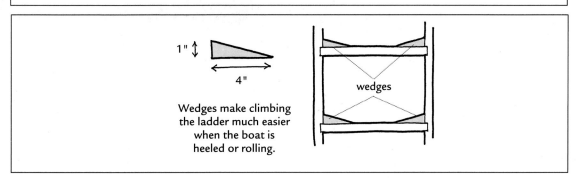

1" ↕
4"

Wedges make climbing the ladder much easier when the boat is heeled or rolling.

wedges

A seaworthy companionway ladder

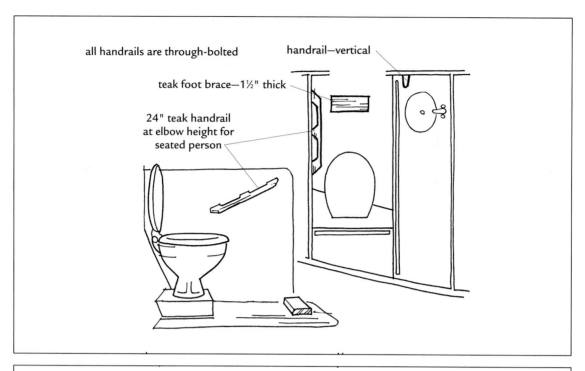

all handrails are through-bolted

handrail—vertical

teak foot brace—1½" thick

24" teak handrail
at elbow height for
seated person

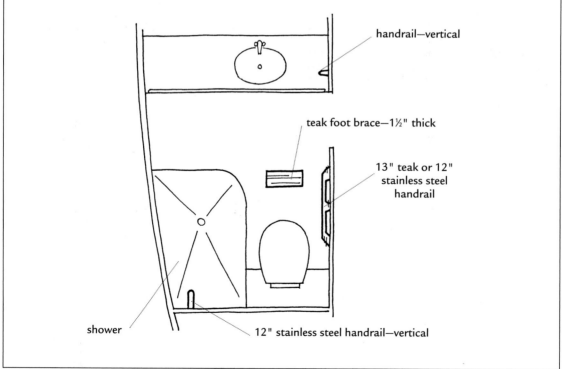

handrail—vertical

teak foot brace—1½" thick

13" teak or 12"
stainless steel
handrail

shower

12" stainless steel handrail—vertical

Grab bars in the head

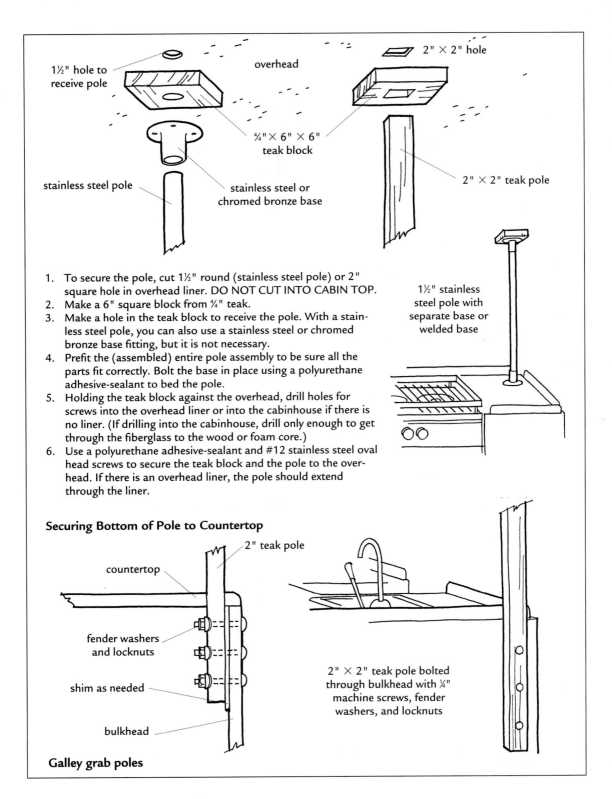

1½" hole to receive pole

overhead

2" × 2" hole

¼" × 6" × 6" teak block

stainless steel pole

stainless steel or chromed bronze base

2" × 2" teak pole

1½" stainless steel pole with separate base or welded base

1. To secure the pole, cut 1½" round (stainless steel pole) or 2" square hole in overhead liner. DO NOT CUT INTO CABIN TOP.
2. Make a 6" square block from ¼" teak.
3. Make a hole in the teak block to receive the pole. With a stainless steel pole, you can also use a stainless steel or chromed bronze base fitting, but it is not necessary.
4. Prefit the (assembled) entire pole assembly to be sure all the parts fit correctly. Bolt the base in place using a polyurethane adhesive-sealant to bed the pole.
5. Holding the teak block against the overhead, drill holes for screws into the overhead liner or into the cabinhouse if there is no liner. (If drilling into the cabinhouse, drill only enough to get through the fiberglass to the wood or foam core.)
6. Use a polyurethane adhesive-sealant and #12 stainless steel oval head screws to secure the teak block and the pole to the overhead. If there is an overhead liner, the pole should extend through the liner.

Securing Bottom of Pole to Countertop

countertop

2" teak pole

fender washers and locknuts

shim as needed

bulkhead

2" × 2" teak pole bolted through bulkhead with ¼" machine screws, fender washers, and locknuts

Galley grab poles

GRAB POLES

On many modern cruising boats, the main cabin has been designed to provide a sense of openness or space. Moreover, particularly on larger boats, the cabin is in fact quite large. While this is great in a calm anchorage, it can be a source of danger at sea unless there are adequate and sturdy places for the crew to hold onto when moving about the cabin.

One of the best means of providing handholds in the main cabin is to erect stout poles that run from cabin sole or countertop to the overhead (see drawing page 87). Ideally, they should be placed so that you can move from one to the other always holding on. While boats differ greatly in their internal geography, it's often possible to install one pole at the forward corner of the galley, a second pole at the table, and a third pole or sturdy vertical handrail at the passageway forward from the main saloon.

Installing poles may require making holes in the countertop, table, or seat back, as well as in the overhead cabin liner, but the job itself should not be difficult. The hardest part is the "thinking" needed before the physical work starts, figuring out the best way to go about the job. Poles can be either 1½-inch diameter stainless steel or teak with a 2-inch cross section. If you associate the poles with a corner of the galley, a table, or a settee back, the actual length of the exposed pole will usually be no more than about 4 feet. In general, the method used to install a galley pole can be applied to other poles as well. The critical element is ensuring that the top and bottom are securely anchored.

INTERIOR HANDRAILS

For the most part (the head being the obvious exception) handrails are not needed in small spaces because you can brace yourself against a wall. In the main cabin, however, where handrails might be useful, they are usually run along the backs of settees or along the sides of the cabinhouse, just below the side windows, where they are so far away from the main passageway as to be useless. The design of some boats, however, particularly those with beams bridging the cabinhouse from port to starboard, provides an opportunity to hang a sturdy handrail from the overhead so that the rail runs within easy reach right along one side or the other of the passageway through the cabin. In addition, the bulkhead or the side of a cabinet immediately adjacent to a door or passageway often offers a convenient location for a handhold.

Glue and screw the teak board with affixed handrail to the overhead using a polyurethane adhesive-sealant and #12 oval-head screws.

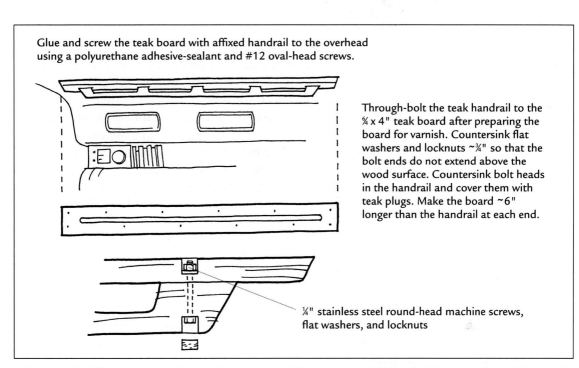

Through-bolt the teak handrail to the ¾ x 4" teak board after preparing the board for varnish. Countersink flat washers and locknuts ~¾" so that the bolt ends do not extend above the wood surface. Countersink bolt heads in the handrail and cover them with teak plugs. Make the board ~6" longer than the handrail at each end.

¼" stainless steel round-head machine screws, flat washers, and locknuts

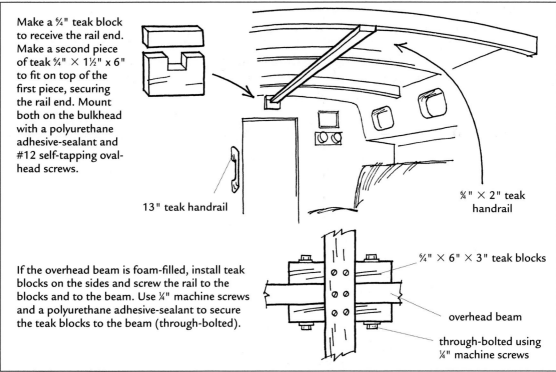

Make a ¾" teak block to receive the rail end. Make a second piece of teak ¾" × 1½" x 6" to fit on top of the first piece, securing the rail end. Mount both on the bulkhead with a polyurethane adhesive-sealant and #12 self-tapping oval-head screws.

13" teak handrail

¾" × 2" teak handrail

¾" × 6" × 3" teak blocks

overhead beam

through-bolted using ¼" machine screws

If the overhead beam is foam-filled, install teak blocks on the sides and screw the rail to the blocks and to the beam. Use ¼" machine screws and a polyurethane adhesive-sealant to secure the teak blocks to the beam (through-bolted).

Overhead handrails

NIGHT LIGHTS

To protect your night vision and be able to see what you're doing while off watch or working in the galley after dark, install red/white cabin lights where lighting is needed at night. These lights usually have two bulbs—one white, the other red—and a switch that lets you use each bulb independently. We have these combination lights in the galley, the head, and the forward cabin, but not in the main salon, where we rely on spillover from the galley light. We also have a flashlight with a red filter for use in the cockpit or on deck.

You can also install low-wattage red night-lights to light the passageways at night so that someone waking at night can move through the boat without turning on an overhead light—analogous to the night-lights many of us have in strategic locations in our homes on land. I suggest using the Sea Dog small-boat vertical sidelight (#400165-1) with a red lens about 6 inches above the cabin sole on the base of berths in sleeping cabins and on a settee base in the main cabin. The Sea Dog light has a stamped stainless steel housing, has not been approved for use as a navigation light by the U.S. Coast Guard, and draws only 0.25 amps; for all of these reasons it sells for only about $20 per pair. To get two red lights, order a set of replacement lenses and swap the green lens that comes in one of the lights for a replacement red lens.

SLEEPING SAFETY

The basic requirement for sleeping safety is staying in your berth. If the berths you'll be using for sleeping while sailing offshore do not have leeboards or lee cloths to keep the occupants from rolling out of bed if the boat lurches suddenly, it would be worthwhile installing one or the other. Leeboards should extend about 8 inches above the mattress, and you'll need a cutout to make it easier to get in and out of the berth. If you don't want permanently installed leeboards, you can design a system that lets you use the leeboards at sea and stow them under the mattress when they're not needed.

Lee cloths, which are even more conveniently stowed under the mattress when not in use, should be long enough to extend from the mid-thigh to the armpit of the occupant of the berth. Lee cloths must be made of sturdy stuff, stoutly reinforced along the top and around any grommets used to secure them. You'll also need sturdy, through-bolted eyes somewhere above the berth to secure the lee cloths when they're in use. If your boat's geography permits access to the underside of the bolts fastening your genoa track to the deck, you may be able to replace three or four nuts on those bolt ends with stainless

Leeboards and lee cloths

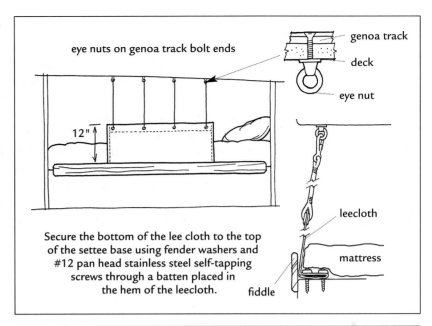

eye nuts on genoa track bolt ends

genoa track

deck

eye nut

12"

leecloth

mattress

Secure the bottom of the lee cloth to the top of the settee base using fender washers and #12 pan head stainless steel self-tapping screws through a batten placed in the hem of the leecloth.

fiddle

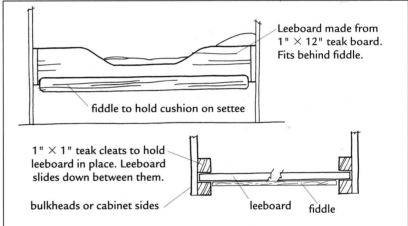

Leeboard made from 1" × 12" teak board. Fits behind fiddle.

fiddle to hold cushion on settee

1" × 1" teak cleats to hold leeboard in place. Leeboard slides down between them.

bulkheads or cabinet sides

leeboard   fiddle

steel eye nuts. Alternatively, you can install eye bolts in the bulkheads at the foot and head of the berth and run a bolt rope through the hem of the lee cloth, securing the rope ends to the eye bolts.

KEEPING THE OCEAN OUTSIDE THE BOAT

It may not be obvious at first that you need to do anything to help keep the ocean out of your boat. Most boats, however, have one or more points of vulnerability. It may be windows, companionways, cockpit lockers, ventilators, through-hull fittings, even anchor lockers. But if you assume that the worst might happen—that your boat might be rolled severely by a rogue wave—and try to eliminate vulnerabilities, not only will your boat be more seaworthy but you and your crew will rest more comfortably.

ANCHOR LOCKERS

The advent of foredeck anchor locker hatches has been a boon for convenience but poses at least one downside for offshore sailors. For many years the drains on those lockers were made so small that the least bit of dirt would clog them. Today some of the drains are larger but still easily blocked by the anchor chain and nylon rode. The potential problem is an anchor locker filled with 25 to 50 gallons or more of water at about 8 pounds per gallon—a lot of undesirable extra weight in the bow at any time but especially in foul weather, when the problem is most likely to occur. (That's one of Murphy's laws: Problems always occur at the worst possible time—or something like that.)

If your boat has a foredeck anchor locker, you might first check the drains. There should be at least two ½- to ¾-inch drain holes covered by stainless steel or chrome-plated brass clamshell vents to help reduce the inflow of water when you're under way. The size of the drain holes is important not so much for how fast they will let water drain out as for their resistance to plugging; a bigger hole is less likely to become plugged.

One hole should be located at the bottom of the locker, the other about halfway up. Both should be on the side of the hull, not through the stem. If you have to make new drain holes in your anchor locker or enlarge existing ones, I recommend against drilling the holes until after you have bought the clamshell vents to cover them so that you can be sure the hole size fits the vent. Having the vents in hand will also help you place the holes. Ideally, the hole should fit near the back of the vent (away from the mouth).

If you do have to drill any new holes in your hull, be sure to seal the fiberglass edges by coating the inside surface of each hole with epoxy resin. In fact, it's worth putting on two coats. Perko makes chrome-plated brass clamshell vents in two sizes (PER 315 001C and 002C); Sea Dog makes stainless steel midget vents (#SDL 331360 and 331370) in similar sizes.

In addition to providing adequate drains for your anchor locker, it's worthwhile trying to minimize the amount of water that can get into the locker around your foredeck hatch. It may be difficult to get a good seal by cementing the usual foam gasket on the underside of the hatch.

Anchor locker drains and hatch gaskets

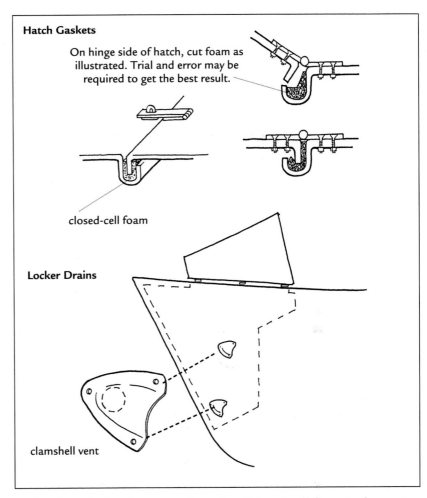

Hatch Gaskets

On hinge side of hatch, cut foam as illustrated. Trial and error may be required to get the best result.

closed-cell foam

Locker Drains

clamshell vent

A simpler solution is to put a fat strip of closed-cell foam in the groove surrounding the hatch opening, close the hatch firmly over the foam, and latch it shut securely before heading out to sea. The edge of the hatch will compress the foam, sealing the perimeter. You can also use a larger piece of closed-cell foam to plug the opening provided for the anchor rode on its way into the locker. That foam also will be compressed and held in place by the closed and latched hatch. If you stow these foam pieces in their own bag in a locker when not needed for passagemaking, they'll last a lot longer than if you just leave them in place whether you need them or not.

COCKPIT BILGE PUMP

If your boat does not have a manual bilge pump that can be operated from the cockpit, you really need to install one—even if you have a good electric bilge pump. The cockpit pump is a backup in case you get a leak that the electric pump—or your batteries—can't handle. The cockpit pump won't handle catastrophic leaks, but it should be able to keep ahead of minor leakage. Moreover, it'll work even if you lose electricity. You can also turn off the electric pump during an ocean passage and use the cockpit pump to monitor leakage by pumping the bilge manually at regular intervals and counting the number of strokes required before you start sucking air. If, on the other hand, you let the electric bilge pump handle the job automatically, a worsening leak may well go undetected until it has reached serious proportions and is too much for your electric pump to handle.

COCKPIT DRAINS

If your boat has an enclosed cockpit, the odds are good that the drains are inadequate for ocean sailing. The problem for aft cockpit boats is that if you are offshore in heavy weather, the cockpit can easily be filled by a wave breaking or slopping over your stern or quarter. If that should happen, you'll want the cockpit drains to carry the water away as quickly as possible. Drains of 1 or even 1½ inches just won't do the job, even on small boats. I'd suggest looking into the feasibility of replacing them with 2-inch drains with the hoses crossed to prevent water from flooding back into the cockpit when the boat is heeled. Use bronze through-hulls and bronze ball cocks so that you can close off the through-hulls if necessary—even if they emerge above the waterline. Also, no matter what size your cockpit drains are, remove the strainer plates that cover the drains in the cockpit before setting out. Those plates will reduce water flow through your drains by 50 percent or more.

COCKPIT LOCKERS

If your cockpit is filled with water, how much of that water will flood into your cockpit lockers and on into your bilge? On some boats the locker hatches extend almost down to the cockpit sole. On most boats there is no seal between the cockpit locker hatch and the locker opening. If either of these arrangements is the case on your boat, see if you can figure out a way to use closed-cell foam to ensure that when the locker hatches are closed, the seal around the edges of those hatches will keep most if not all of the water in a flooded cockpit in the cockpit and not let it spread to the locker. Also, make sure that you can keep the cockpit hatches closed. The closure doesn't have to be fancy. We use simple brass snaphooks through the hasps to make sure our cockpit lockers will stay closed.

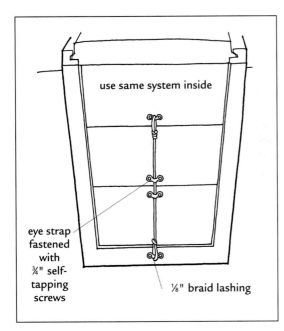

use same system inside

eye strap
fastened
with
¾" self-
tapping
screws

⅛" braid lashing

Securing hatchboards

HATCHBOARDS

Will your hatchboards stay in place in a knock-down or worse? Many will fall out, leaving the boat vulnerable to flooding through the companionway. It doesn't take much effort, however, to make sure your companionway hatchboards will stay put even if the boat does a 360. First, install eye straps near the bottom center on both sides of each hatchboard. Next, install eye straps just below the companionway, again inside and out. To secure whatever hatchboards you have in place, run a lashing from the eye strap below the companionway to the eye strap of the topmost hatchboard, pull it tight, and secure it with a couple of half hitches—it will be easy to untie, but not so easy that it might come loose accidentally. Having eye straps on both sides of the hatchboards and below the companionway inside and out allows you to secure the hatchboards from the cabin as well as from the cockpit.

THROUGH-HULL FITTINGS

If your boat is equipped with plastic seacocks, I recommend replacing them with bronze ball valves. Although some plastic ball valves meet American Boat and Yacht Council (ABYC) standards, I prefer the ruggedness of bronze valves and the knowledge that I don't have to worry about using too much force and breaking the handle or shaft. If a problem develops at sea and you have to close a seacock in an emergency, you want something that will take whatever force the crew's adrenaline rush throws at it. A quality bronze ball valve with a stainless steel handle will do that.

Further, if your through-hull fittings above the waterline (AWL) do not have seacocks on them or are not true through-hull fittings, they should be replaced as well. Some AWL through-hulls are created by epoxying a fiberglass or plastic tube into a hole drilled through the hull. Most often there is a backing block on the inside of the hull. Boatbuilders say that it's okay to use such through-hull systems because they are located above the waterline. This may be true when the boat's at rest, but these same through-hulls may be well below the water's surface when the boat is under sail. While these through-hulls may be acceptable for inshore waters where help is usually nearby, they are not acceptable offshore where getting help is more problematical. Pru-

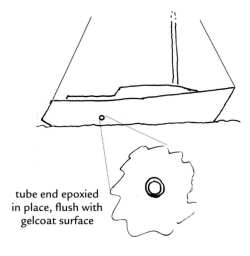

tube end epoxied
in place, flush with
gelcoat surface

When removing old tube, try to
retain the wood (or fiberglass)
block mounted on hull inside.

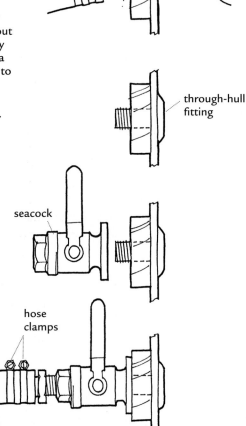

through-hull
fitting

seacock

hose
clamps

1. Use hole saw of same size as outer diameter of through-hull you will be installing to cut out the tube, continuing the new hole completely through the wood backing block. Hint: jam a piece of wood into the existing through-hull to make it easier to use the hole saw.

2. Seal fiberglass sides of hole with epoxy resin.

3. Install bronze through-hull fitting, bedding well with a sealant for use below the waterline.

4. Wrap threads of through-hull fitting with Teflon tape.

5. Install bronze seacock on through-hull fitting. Secure base to wood block using #12 stainless steel pan head self-tapping screws with flat washers under screw heads.

6. Wrap thread of pipe-to-hose adaptor and screw into open end of seacock.

7. Connect hose, securing with two stainless steel hose clamps.

Replacing the through-hull tube with a bronze through-hull and seacock

dence and good seamanship suggest that you should have a way of closing all through-hulls, even those above the waterline, before heading out to sea. The work involved is usually straightforward.

WINDOWS

Windows can be a boat's single most vulnerable point in serious weather when it comes to keeping the ocean outside of the boat. You need to ask yourself whether your boat's windows could withstand the effects of the boat's being thrown on its beam ends by a rogue sea in the midst of a gale. It's probably not a question you can answer, but experience suggests that the answer would be negative for many boats built over the past 30 years or so. And the reason is simple: most sailors don't need or want bulletproof windows. Therefore, with a few notable exceptions, the market doesn't provide them.

The most secure windows are opening ports framed in cast bronze, stainless steel, or aluminum alloy with screw-down dogs to hold them tightly closed. They are sturdy and generally relatively small. Also high on the list are heavy-duty Lexan or plate-glass fixed ports that are fastened to the cabinhouse with bolts every 4 inches or so around the circumference. They may or may not have sturdy metal frames. Small fixed ports are best. As windows become larger, they also become more vulnerable.

If your boat's opening ports are made of plastic or if your fixed ports are not well bolted to the cabinhouse or are somewhat large, consider upgrading your windows before heading out to sea. You have three basic options: replacing your existing ports, making your existing ports more secure, or adding storm windows.

For opening ports, the best option is to replace plastic ports with sturdy cast bronze, stainless steel, or aluminum alloy ports. Choose ports that have traditional screw-down dogs and metal (not plastic) hinges. Stainless steel and bronze opening ports made by ABI, bronze ports made by Sea Fit, and Bomar's series 200 traditional cast almag opening ports are either standard items or can be specially ordered at major marine stores.

For fixed ports—assuming your existing windows don't leak—the best option often is to bolt storm windows of ⅜- or even ½-inch Lexan over your existing ports. Although the details of the job will vary from boat to boat, the general scheme for making storm windows consists of making a paper or cardboard template of the window, then making a storm window frame, and finally installing the frame permanently on the cabinhouse. For passages, the storm win-

1. Make cardboard template of window to receive storm window.
2. Make teak frame to surround template. Check fit around window before gluing (epoxy) and screwing pieces together. Recheck fit on window.
3. Make second, identical teak frame.
4. Make cardboard template of teak frame. Use that template to have Lexan cut to correct size and fit.
5. Cut drains in bottom of outside surface (Lexan side) of "inside" frame. This frame will be permanently mounted on cabinhouse.
6. Assemble storm window "sandwich." Holding it securely (use masking tape to bind pieces together), drill ¼" holes through all layers on all four sides. Insert ¼" round head machine screws in each hole as drilled to help hold layers in position. Thereafter, drill holes all around, about 4" apart.
7. Remove Lexan from sandwich and enlarge holes in Lexan to ⁵⁄₁₆".
8. Position "inside" frame over window on cabinhouse. Use double-stick carpet tape to hold frame in position. Drill ¼" holes through cabinhouse in all four sides, using holes in frame as drill guides. Insert first four machine screws and tighten nuts. Drill remaining holes.
9. Remove frame from cabinhouse. Use ⁹⁄₃₂" bit to enlarge holes in cabinhouse. Swab holes with epoxy resin to seal fiberglass edges and wood core.
10. Install "inside" frame, bedding well with silicone or acrylic caulk. Bed bolts and bolt heads with same caulk.
11. Apply finish to teak frame (varnish, oil, Cetol, etc.).
12. Remove all bolts and use longer bolts to install Lexan storm window and teak "outside" frame over permanently installed "inside" frame. Caulk (bed) only around bolt holes and under bolt heads.

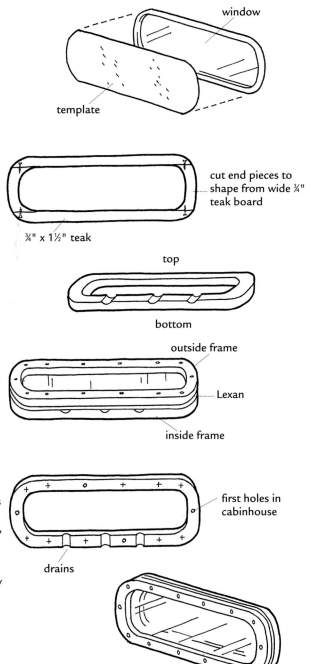

window

template

cut end pieces to shape from wide ¾" teak board

¾" x 1½" teak

top

bottom

outside frame

Lexan

inside frame

first holes in cabinhouse

drains

Storm windows

dow is installed over the teak frame. It's worthwhile running a small bead of silicone caulk along the outside of the joints between the teak frames and the Lexan to help protect against leakage. That surface caulking is easily cleaned off when the storm window is removed for stowage until the next passage.

Finishing off the interior bolt ends resulting from installing the storm window frames may be your biggest challenge. A teak frame similar to that made for the exterior might be in order, though it could be made with thinner stock. Also, if you cut your machine screws to length, you may be able to use barrel nuts or cap nuts to provide a finished look to the bolt ends. It's best to figure out how you'll finish off the bolts ends before you start the project.

PREPARING FOR FOUL WEATHER

One of the best pieces of advice I have ever received regarding ocean sailing is to prepare for foul weather *before* you head out to sea. This advice is equally sound whether you are headed out onto the ocean, a lake, or a nearby bay, sound, or river. The degree of preparation may differ, but the principle's the same. It's a bit late, for example, to start securing things on deck, in lockers, or down below when you see an unpredicted thunderstorm, squall line, or gale rushing down on you. Shortening sail and clearing the cockpit will probably keep you busy enough.

ANCHOR SECURITY

It may sound like overkill, but it's a good idea to secure your anchors in the bow roller to eliminate any possibility they'll break loose (see page 100). One way to secure your anchors is to lash the shanks of the anchors to a cleat placed between them on the foredeck, as described under Anchor Cleats in chapter 3. An alternative is to install anchor-shaft brackets (e.g., Spartan SPN B220 or B223) on the foredeck. These brackets will hold the shanks of your anchors securely so that the anchors themselves cannot move. We go one step further, tying a ¼-inch rope tail to the eye at the bend of the anchor shank (just above the flukes) and securing that with a clove hitch to the bow rail—always, even in protected waters. When anchoring, we use that short line to attach the line to our anchor buoy.

anchor-shaft
bracket

CABINET AND LOCKER SECURITY

Your locker and cabinet doors must remain closed even if the boat's motion throws their contents against the doors. This is true inshore as well as offshore. On the open ocean, it's helpful if cabinets and lockers remain closed (instead of spilling their contents all over) even if the boat does a 360-degree roll.

For lockers behind a settee back or under seat cushions, use ¼- or ⁵⁄₁₆-inch shock cord to keep the lids on. By drilling holes on each side of the locker's lift-out lid or hinged door, you can thread shock cord through the first hole, knot the end with a figure-eight knot on the inside of the locker, thread the other end through a hole on the other side of the door, stretch it tight, and tie off the second end with a figure-eight knot. Shock cord stretched across the door (two shock cords if the lid is not hinged) will keep it closed even in extreme circumstances.

Cabinet doors may require additional hardware. For example, I don't trust the finger latches often found on boat cabinet doors for offshore sailing, especially if those lockers are used to hold hard goods (canned food, bottles, etc.) that can fall against the door and trip the latch, knocking the door open. Either a small door hook and eye or a cupboard bolt (Sea Dog #222380-1) will provide the extra security needed. The shock-cord system described above is also

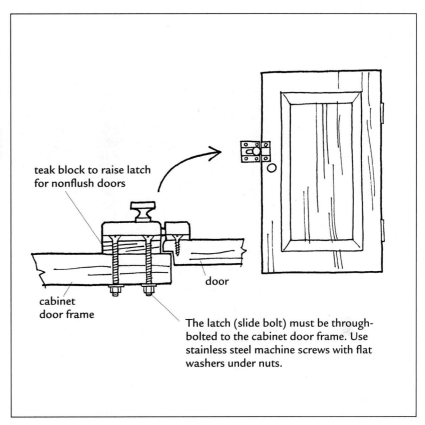

teak block to raise latch
for nonflush doors

door

cabinet
door frame

The latch (slide bolt) must be through-
bolted to the cabinet door frame. Use
stainless steel machine screws with flat
washers under nuts.

effective. The shock cord can be removed in inshore waters, where it is not needed. For aesthetic reasons, you may want to put teak plugs in the holes for the shock cords. Put the plugs in without glue so that they can easily be pushed out when the shock cord is needed again. A dab of varnish on the plug ends will make them almost invisible.

CABIN SOLE HATCHES

For sailing offshore, it's also a good idea to have positive latches on all hatches in the cabin sole. Turning lock lift handles (ABI #2020) will fill the need nicely. The latch plate and handle assembly is mortised into the hatch, and the locking arm can be adjusted to fit your cabin sole. If your cabin sole hatches are not hinged (most are not), you will also need to install a passive latch to secure the end opposite the turning latch. One half of a standard indoor brass door hinge works well for this purpose. The rolled edge of the hinge will slip right under the hatch frame. The good news is that the hinges are inexpensive. The turning lock lift handles retail for about $40.

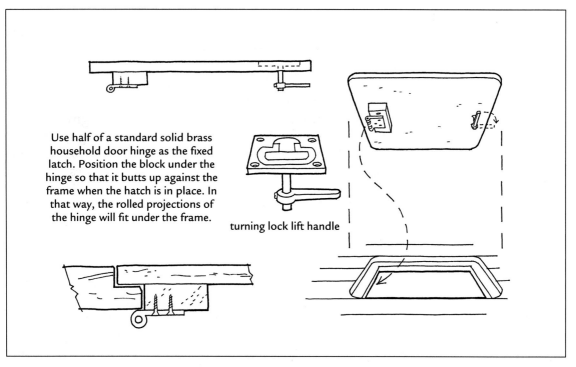

Use half of a standard solid brass household door hinge as the fixed latch. Position the block under the hinge so that it butts up against the frame when the hatch is in place. In that way, the rolled projections of the hinge will fit under the frame.

turning lock lift handle

Securing cabin sole hatchboards

FURLING-MAINSAIL BACKUP

If your furling-mainsail system does not have a track for a backup mainsail, it's worth having a track installed, much as you would for a storm trysail (see Storm Trysail, beginning on page 107). The track should extend to the height of your mainsail when it has a single reef in it. Then, you can either have a somewhat smaller backup mainsail made or buy a used mainsail from a sail broker and have it modified for use with your new sail track.

This same track can be used for a storm trysail, but a trysail is not much good as a backup for your furling mainsail. The center of effort on the trysail is too far forward for it to be of much use in moderate or light winds—unless, of course, you don't want to sail closer to the wind than a beam reach.

DINGHY STOWAGE

In protected waters one can tow a dinghy safely as long as the wind doesn't become very strong. When you leave protected waters, however, the dinghy should be stowed either on deck or down below. Otherwise you run the very real risk of losing your dinghy if the weather deteriorates.

A hard dinghy can be safely stowed on deck for most passages using the chocks-and-tie-down system described under Livability in chapter 2. Stowing an inflatable on deck when sailing offshore, however, assumes no more than a 24- to 48-hour passage, when you can be reasonably secure in the weather. If your passage will be longer than that, you should stow the inflatable below. If you have a cockpit locker large enough for the rolled-up dinghy, that's a good place to put it so long as the dinghy's not sharing space with sharp items that could damage its tubes. On *Sea Sparrow*, our inflatable is stowed in the forward cabin for long passages. After we turn the cushions up against the hull, the rolled-up inflatable fits the V-berth quite nicely, and the 4-inch fiddle that normally holds the cushions in place keeps the dinghy safely where we put it.

LIFE RAFT

A life raft is recommended equipment on any well-found boat headed out to sea. If you will be doing much ocean sailing, you'll save money in the long run by purchasing your own raft. For an occasional passage, you may be able to rent a life raft. In either case, however, you'll need a place to stow it, probably on deck (see page 104). After all, a life raft stowed in a locker and eventually covered by a lot of other gear won't do you much good if you need it in a hurry.

One method of deck stowage, particularly if the raft is contained in a hard case, is to use a stainless steel frame with a quick-release mechanism. The manufacturer of your life raft probably offers a frame designed specifically for the raft. An alternative is to through-bolt six folding padeyes to the deck and lash your raft in place. When the raft is stowed ashore (or between rentals), the folding padeyes—unlike a frame—are conveniently out of the way. When preparing for sea you can lash the raft securely in place using ¼-inch, low-stretch braided polyester line, which is sturdy enough for the job yet small enough to be cut easily using a good pair of snips if the raft is needed. You will need to check the lashings daily, however, to be sure that they do not loosen. You will also need a pair of scissors or snips specifically for the life raft and kept readily accessible in the cockpit. Try the scissors or snips out ahead of time to be sure they will cut your lashings easily when they are wet as well as when they are dry. Note: scissors, or better still, snips, are preferable to a knife for this purpose because they are less likely to cause personal injury or accidental damage to the raft in the urgency of the moment.

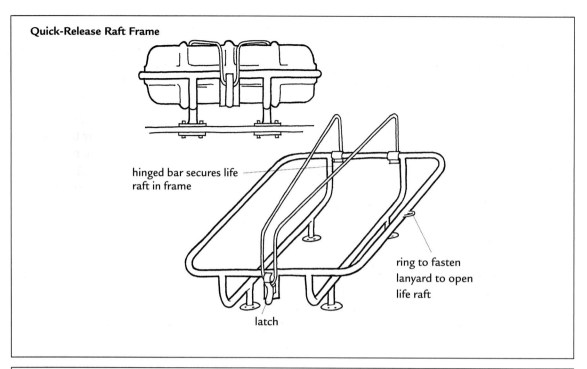

Quick-Release Raft Frame

hinged bar secures life raft in frame

ring to fasten lanyard to open life raft

latch

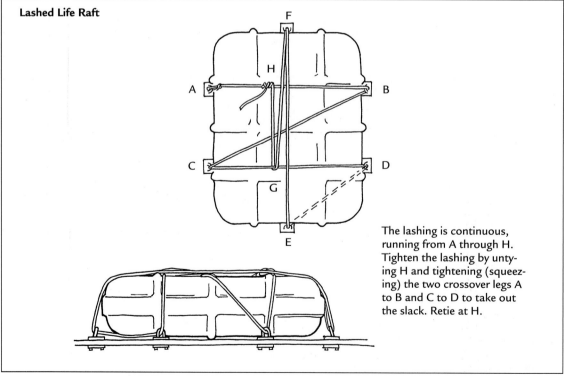

Lashed Life Raft

F

H

A   B

C   D

G

E

The lashing is continuous, running from A through H. Tighten the lashing by untying H and tightening (squeezing) the two crossover legs A to B and C to D to take out the slack. Retie at H.

Life raft frame and lashing systems

MAINSAIL REEFING

If your mainsail is rigged to be reefed from the cockpit, you are well advised to install winches and cleats on the mast as a backup so that you can work the halyard and the reef line from the mast when sailing offshore. In heavy weather, sails often won't slide easily down the mast but must be helped down by hand. Also, if your mainsail does not have them, ask your sailmaker to add grommets for reef points to your sail so that you can tie in your reef to secure the reefed portion of the sail. In stronger winds, the flap of sail formed when you take a reef using your jiffy or slab reefing system can flog itself to death if left unsecured. Rather than tying individual reef points, however, run a continuous line from the boom through the grommet nearest the sail's leech, then under the sail (between the boom and sail) and to the next grommet, and so on, in a lacing manner. After taking in the reef, you can contain the flap of sail by pulling in on this line and securing it. Using a continuous line to tie in the reef has two advantages: you don't have to walk out the length of the boom on the cabinhouse to tie individual reef points, and you

**Tying in reefs—
the easy way**

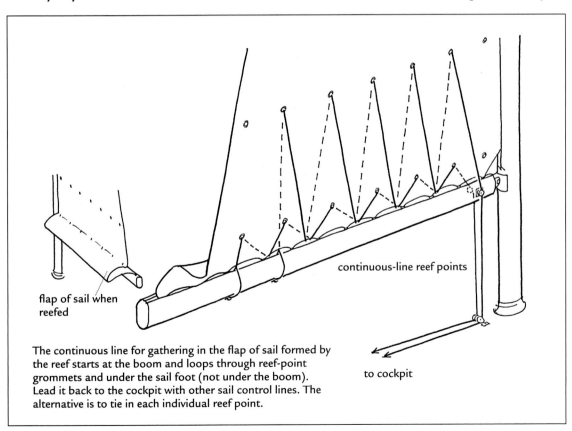

flap of sail when reefed

continuous-line reef points

The continuous line for gathering in the flap of sail formed by the reef starts at the boom and loops through reef-point grommets and under the sail foot (not under the boom). Lead it back to the cockpit with other sail control lines. The alternative is to tie in each individual reef point.

to cockpit

can't forget to untie one reef point and tear your sail as a result. A good set of lazy jacks will also help secure the flap of sail.

SETTEES

If your settees do not have at least 3-inch fiddles to hold the cushions in place, consider carefully what will keep your seat cushions where they belong in rough weather and an active seaway. A hook-and-loop fastener such as Velcro will probably work if there's enough of it. But fiddles have been used for decades, if not centuries, for one primary reason: they do the job. The fiddles should be half as tall as your cushions are thick if they are to hold the cushions in place when the boat rolls heavily.

If your settees pull out to provide a wider sleeping berth, check to be sure that you have some way to keep them from sliding out on their own when the boat is rolled. The simplest way I know to do this is to use carriage bolts as pins to hold the settee seats in place. On *Sea Sparrow*, the pins have two positions so that we can lock the settee bases in place both when they are pushed in for use as seats and when they are pulled out as berths.

Locking pins and fiddles for settees or berths

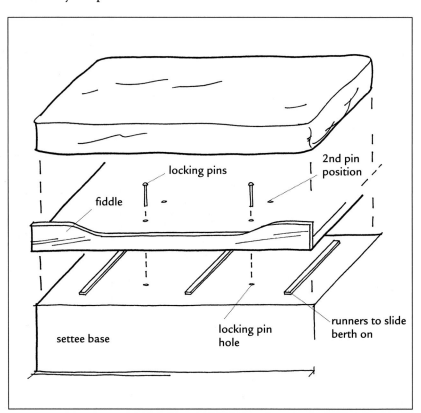

CHAPTER FOUR

If your mast does not have a separate track for a storm trysail, that's something you really should remedy. The midst of a gale is no time to be removing your mainsail to free up a mast track so that you can hoist a storm trysail. Installing track for a trysail requires spending several hours in a bosun's chair (unless you have the mast pulled for the job) and a bit of patience, but it's not difficult. You simply have to

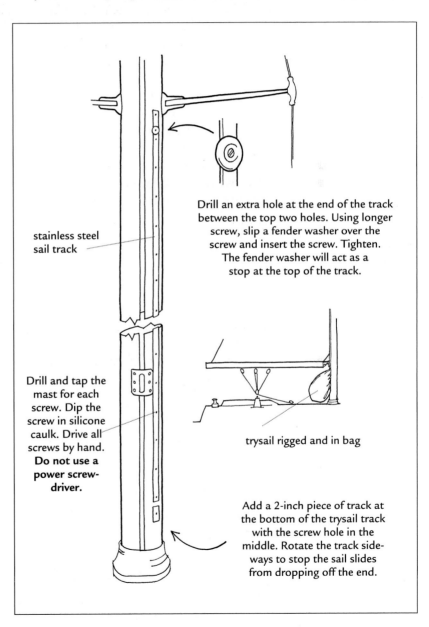

stainless steel
sail track

Drill an extra hole at the end of the track between the top two holes. Using longer screw, slip a fender washer over the screw and insert the screw. Tighten. The fender washer will act as a stop at the top of the track.

Drill and tap the mast for each screw. Dip the screw in silicone caulk. Drive all screws by hand. **Do not use a power screwdriver.**

trysail rigged and in bag

Add a 2-inch piece of track at the bottom of the trysail track with the screw hole in the middle. Rotate the track sideways to stop the sail slides from dropping off the end.

Storm-trysail rig

drill and tap a lot of holes in your mast and use small, round head machine screws dipped in silicone caulk to fasten the track to the mast. (The silicone helps prevent galvanic corrosion between the stainless steel screws and the aluminum mast.) Run the track up to the first set of spreaders about 1 to 1½ inches to the side of your primary sail track. If possible, also extend it down to within a foot or so of the cabinhouse (deck). This will allow you to put the trysail on the track and keep it bagged and ready to use at the foot of the mast when you're at sea. We've had occasion to use our trysail only twice over the years, but we were glad both times that it was rigged ahead of time.

V-BERTH

You can put your V-berth to good use at sea by converting it to storage. The odds are that no one will sleep there anyway. There's too much motion, and it can be really noisy up there because of the constant sound of the bow going through the water. By installing sturdy eye straps or padeyes on the V-berth's base (under the mattress), and lifting the cushions to the side so they lean up against the hull, you can secure all kinds of gear on the V-berth base using the eye straps or padeyes to lash things down. Not only do we put the inflatable dinghy there when going offshore but we also use the V-berth to stow sails and tubs of various gear that's useful in an anchorage but seldom, if ever, needed at sea.

PROTECTING RIG AND PROPELLER

Protecting the rig begins with having it inspected by a rigger well before setting off to sea. While modern stainless steel wire generally will last a long time, it is affected by fatigue as well as by corrosion and pitting, particularly at the lower terminals. And it can fail suddenly—usually at the worst possible time (e.g., in the midst of a gale) because that's when the stresses on the rig are highest. Moreover, depending upon the size of your boat and where you use it, swaged terminals and the ball-head ends of rod rigging and ball-end terminals may also fail catastrophically. Swaged terminals may need to be replaced after as few as 3 years, but they may last as many as 20 years. They tend to last longer on boats of 30 feet or less than they do on larger boats because the stresses on the rigging are less. Swaged fittings also tend to last longer on boats used in fresh water and, next best, northern coastal waters than on boats used in southern waters because the warmer temperatures and higher salt content of southern waters accelerate aging, particularly of lower (deck-level) terminals.

Rod rigging may last as long as 10 years, but it too must be watched for signs of fatigue. Rod rigging tends to fail at the junction between the ball and the rod. Similarly, ball-end terminals on wire rigging tend to fail between the ball and the shank of the terminal.

ADDING AN INNER FORESTAY

If your sloop or ketch has a single headsail, adding an inner forestay can greatly improve your boat's ability to sail in stronger winds, particularly if you need to sail upwind. As you reef the mainsail, you move that sail's center of effort forward. As you reduce the size of your headsail, its center of effort is also moved forward. As a result, not only will it become increasingly difficult for you to sail upwind but you may develop an unbalanced helm even on a beam reach. By adding an inner forestay, you can douse your headsail completely and sail with a double- or even triple-reefed mainsail and a staysail or storm jib on the inner forestay. Because the sails are closer together, your sails will be better balanced and you'll be better able to sail upwind if necessary.

Adding an inner forestay is best left to a rigger. Although modifying the mast for the inner forestay is straightforward, securing the deck fitting for attaching the bottom of the stay is often more involved.

Adding an inner forestay may also mean installing running backstays to counteract the forward pull of the stay on the middle of the mast. Running backs are easily installed by adding tangs to the mast at about the same height as the head of the inner forestay. (A compression tube will be required through the mast for the bolt used to secure the tangs.) At the other end, rig two heavy-duty padeyes (with large backing plates) on the stern or transom just port and starboard of the backstay chainplate (or inboard of the split backstay chainplates) and use a two-part block and tackle to tension and slack off on the running backstays as needed.

Some sailors are put off by the complications of using running backstays—switching from one to the other when tacking and stowing them when they're not needed. While there's no way to get around the need to switch from one running back to the other when tacking, it's worth noting that you don't normally do much tacking in the conditions in which you most need the running backstays. As for stowing them when they're not needed, that's a problem with an easy solution.

Adding an inner forestay

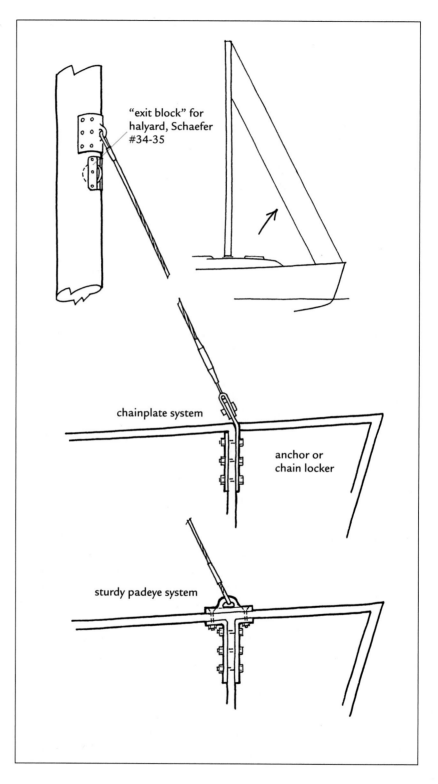

"exit block" for halyard, Schaefer #34-35

chainplate system

anchor or chain locker

sturdy padeye system

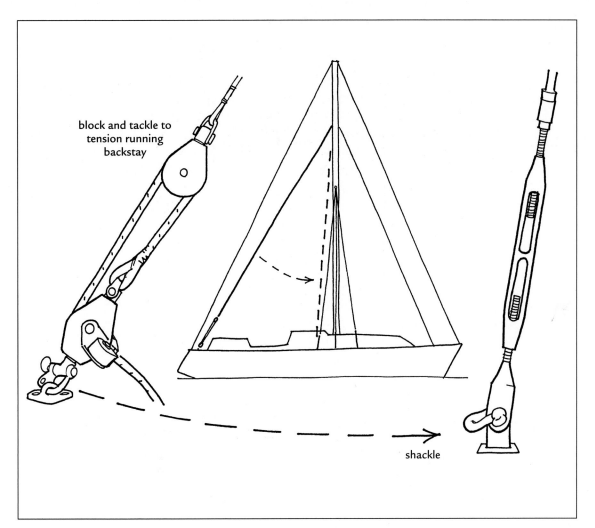

block and tackle to
tension running
backstay

shackle

Running backstays   Install shackles on the chainplates of your aft lower shrouds port
and starboard and snap shackles to the bottom ends of the block and
tackles used to adjust the running backs. By the simple expedient of
making the wire portion of your running backstays short enough to
end about 2 feet above the deck when they are pulled forward to the
lower shrouds, you can use your snap shackles to move the block and
tackles from the stern to the shackles on the lower-shroud chainplates
and tie them off when they're not needed.

BACKUP HEADSTAY

I know of two different boats that lost their headstays in midocean
with only modest inconvenience to their husband-and-wife crews.
How is that possible? In both instances the crews had prepared for

the eventuality by rigging their boats with backup headstays (see page 113). The backup headstay offers other utility as well for boats with roller-furling jibs; it provides a place to hang a storm jib if you don't have an inner forestay.

The backup headstay probably will not be rigged much of the time. It would interfere with normal use of the jib. Instead, it should be easily rigged and put aside when not needed, stowed near the upper shrouds on one side or the other. This too is an installation that may be best left to a professional rigger. The backup stay should be secured at the top just below the blocks for the main jib halyards. If space permits, the bottom should be secured to the stemhead fitting just back from the headstay. Otherwise a separate attachment plate and fitting will be required. When it is stowed off to the side, the backup headstay can be secured by snagging it in a corkscrew catch located 6 to 12 inches out from the mast on a lower spreader and fastening the bottom to a padeye on deck near the upper-shroud chainplate or to a shackle on that chainplate. On many boats the length of the backup headstay will fit this geometry nicely, and the stay can be tied off to the forward lower shroud to remove any slack.

MULTISPREADER LIGHTWEIGHT MASTS

Many cruising boats of recent years have been delivered with highly tuned, lightweight, multispreader rigs. They contribute to the light-air sailing performance and are well suited for inshore cruising—even for coastal cruising in areas where you're not far from help if it's needed. But for serious ocean sailing, a cruising boat should be forgiving. And the rig should be forgiving as well.

What this boils down to, of course, is that you should consider getting a new mast and standing rigging if your boat has one of those lightweight, multispreader rigs. And while you're at it, specify Norseman or Sta-Lok terminals for all of your standing rigging. They far outlast swaged terminals. The cost of rerigging a 35-foot boat will range from $10,000 to $15,000. For a 40-footer, figure $15,000 to $20,000. What you would gain from that investment would be the peace of mind that comes with knowing you've got a rig designed for the sailing you'll be doing, not one that was designed for racing boats and put on cruising boats for reasons of marketing and cost.

PREVENTERS

Any boat sailing downwind on the ocean or any other large body of water needs some system for preventing accidental jibes caused by

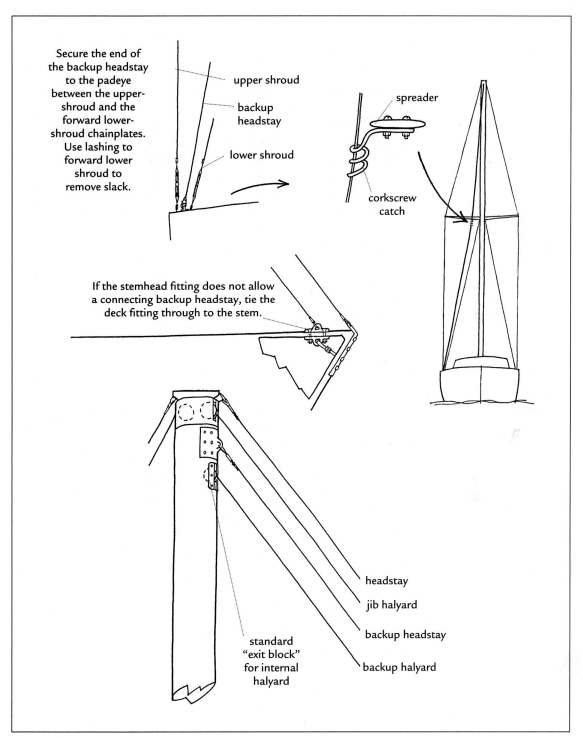

Secure the end of the backup headstay to the padeye between the upper-shroud and the forward lower-shroud chainplates. Use lashing to forward lower shroud to remove slack.

upper shroud

backup headstay

lower shroud

spreader

corkscrew catch

If the stemhead fitting does not allow a connecting backup headstay, tie the deck fitting through to the stem.

headstay

jib halyard

backup headstay

backup halyard

standard "exit block" for internal halyard

Backup headstay

Block and Tackle Preventers

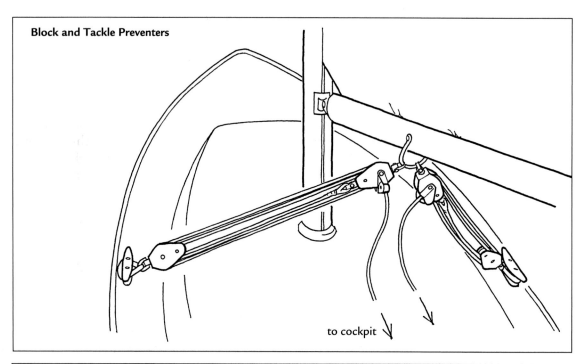

to cockpit

Dutchman Boom Brake

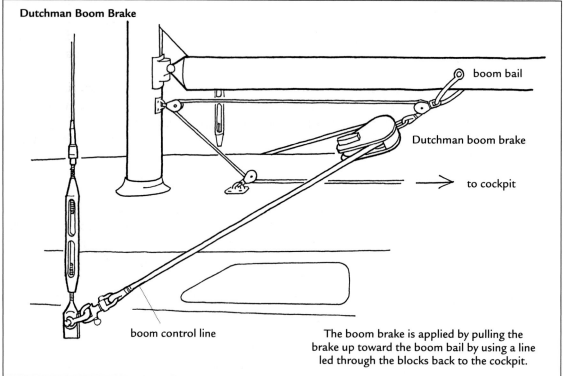

boom bail

Dutchman boom brake

to cockpit

boom control line

The boom brake is applied by pulling the brake up toward the boom bail by using a line led through the blocks back to the cockpit.

Mid-boom preventers

the boat's rolling motion. I can suggest three approaches: use a boom brake; secure the boom to a midship cleat with a combination vang and preventer; or rig true preventers.

The Dutchman boom brake is rigged port and starboard between shackles on the chainplates for the aft lower shrouds, midship cleats, or sturdy padeyes somewhere between the two. The brake itself is suspended from a line through a block on the boom bail, and that line is led forward to the base of the mast and aft to the cockpit. Pulling on the brake line puts tension on the brake mechanism by drawing it back toward the bail—in effect applying the brakes to the boom. Easing pressure on the brake line allows the boom to move. With the brake "set" (the brake line pulled tight and cleated), the boom is prevented from swinging across the boat if you jibe accidentally. By easing the brake, however, you can let the boom cross the boat in a controlled manner. List prices for Dutchman boom brakes suitable for boats in the 26- to 45-foot range are between $180 and $325.

A somewhat cruder way of accomplishing the same things is to use separate block and tackles from the boom bail to the midship cleats or padeyes port and starboard as a boom vang at all times and as a preventer when sailing downwind. While it's possible to make do with a single block and tackle by transferring the rig from side to side each time you tack or jibe, actually getting out on deck and moving it from the windward cleat to the leeward cleat when the boat is heeled well over and a sea is running can be challenging.

A mid-boom preventer works only because modern rigs tend to have short booms and higher hull profiles so that the ends of the booms do not dip into the water as the boat rolls downwind. If they did, the mid-boom preventer could easily result in a broken boom. The traditional preventer, which runs from the end of the boom to a block on the foredeck and back to the cockpit, is better suited to keeping the boom in one piece if its end is caught by a wave.

You can set a traditional preventer easily. First, rig pendants from a bail at the after end of the boom and run them forward along the boom to cleats near the mast. Second, run preventer lines port and starboard from the cockpit to blocks on the bow—perhaps secured to the forward mooring cleats—and then back outside the lifelines to a stanchion, shackle, or cleat amidships. Eyes should be spliced in the midship ends of these lines. When a preventer is needed, remove the appropriate boom pendant from the forward end of the boom and use a bowline to secure it to the eye of the leeward preventer line. Then take in the slack and cleat your preventer in the cockpit.

Traditional end-of-boom preventers

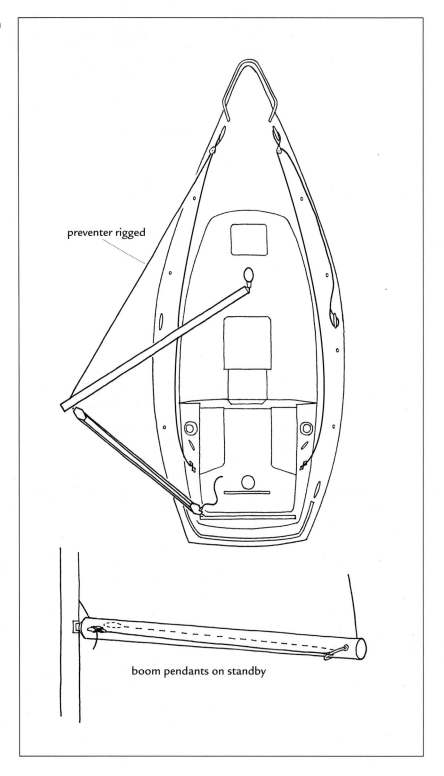

preventer rigged

boom pendants on standby

PROP PROTECTION

Installing cutters on your prop shaft that will cut a rope that otherwise threatens to wrap around your propeller is an anathema in some parts of the United States, but there's a lot of ⅜-inch polypropylene rope floating around the waters of the world. If some of that line fouls your propeller, you could be between a rock and a hard place—literally—if you're relying on your engine to get through a cut or a break in a reef to a safe anchorage. Similarly, a patch of floating weeds can foul your propeller. In fact, we once had to dive on our propeller in the dark when it was fouled by seaweed as we were motoring into a channel through reefs in the Florida Keys to begin an overnight crossing to the Bahama Islands. To avoid situations like that, cruising sailors should consider installing a set of Spurs line and weed cutters.

REPLACING ROD RIGGING OR BALL-END TERMINALS

For long-distance cruising, your rigger may recommend replacing the rod rigging or the ball-end terminals on wire rigging. The reason, as noted earlier, is that the ball ends can break off without warning, causing the rigging to fail. The change to swaged terminals or, preferably, swageless terminals such as Norseman or Sta-Lok can be made using your existing mast by cutting off the top of the mast and installing a new head. Toggles for lower and intermediate shrouds can be installed easily using a bolt and compression tube through the mast. The cost of converting a mast and existing rigging on a 35- to 40-foot boat will be about $5,000. If you also need to replace the rigging, add about $2,000.

Swageless wire terminal

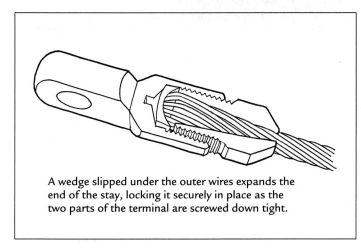

A wedge slipped under the outer wires expands the end of the stay, locking it securely in place as the two parts of the terminal are screwed down tight.

REPLACING SWAGED TERMINALS

If inspection of your rigging reveals small cracks in any of your swaged terminals, replace all of your terminal fittings with Norseman or Sta-Lok swageless terminals. Not only will you then have terminals that will outlast your wire rigging but you'll be able to reuse those terminals when it's time to replace the wire.

This is one rigging job you can do yourself. Installing the swageless fittings is straightforward and does not require any special tools. Extra-long stud terminals are available for use with your turnbuckles to compensate for shortening your wire in cutting off the old swaged fittings. In fact, the hardest part of the job probably will be cutting the existing terminals off the wire and leaving a cleanly cut wire end. Quality wire cutters will do the job; you should have them on the boat anyway if you are sailing offshore so that you can cut away the mast if you lose it. Although the initial cost of swageless fittings is roughly double that of swaged terminals, their lifetime cost likely will be lower.

5

MAKE YOUR BOAT
Sail Faster

A cruising sailboat's speed is a relative matter. You already know, for example, that how fast your boat will sail is limited by the length of its waterline. If your boat has a waterline of 25 feet, unless you start surfing down waves (not recommended), your boat simply won't go through the water faster than about 6.7 knots. For a 30-foot water-line the limit is about 7.3 knots. A 35-foot waterline yields a maximum boat speed of about 7.9 knots. And so on.

One trick naval architects have adopted to add an extra half-knot or so to boat speed is simply to lengthen the waterline. As a result, many of today's designs have reverse transoms and stems almost straight up and down so that in effect the waterline length is almost the same as the boat length. Shallow bilges with relatively flat runs from stem to stern, along with lighter displacements, have yielded boats that will approach their maximum theoretical speeds in lighter winds because there's not as much mass to push through the water.

The question is, however, What can you do to help your boat maximize its performance? Frankly, the best advice I've heard given to cruising sailors who want to improve their boat's performance is to steal a page or two from their racing counterpart's playbook. First, get rid of extraneous weight. Second, look for ways to reduce drag below the waterline. And third, get the best performance possible out of your boat's rig, perhaps even modifying the rig to do that.

TAKING OFF WEIGHT

Cruising boats are like attics, basements, and garages: They accumulate all sorts of gear and equipment. Usually, some of that "stuff" can simply be weeded out and disposed of—a chore worth doing every year. Other gear and supplies may be needed for longer vacation cruises but are completely unnecessary for weekend sailing. Those items can be stored ashore until you prepare for a cruising vacation. Depending upon your boat's water tankage, you may even be able to sail on weekends with less than a full load of water (water weighs about 8 pounds per gallon). Once all the extra weight is taken off the boat, it may float as much as an inch higher on the waterline. If so, you'll notice the difference in performance, especially in light air.

BELOW THE WATERLINE

Once you have made your boat's bottom as smooth as possible, there are only two ways to enhance your boat's performance without major surgery—adding fairing strips to your skeg or keel-hung rudder and getting rid of your fixed-blade propeller. The first will improve your boat's performance only incrementally; the second will probably add a knot of boat speed.

FAIRING STRIPS

If a rudder is mounted behind a full or partial skeg or immediately behind the keel, the simple addition of fairing strips to cover any gap between the skeg (keel) and the rudder will reduce turbulence and, therefore, drag by providing a smooth run for the water as it moves along the keel or skeg and then past the rudder. You can use stainless steel sheet stock for your fairing strips, but the material that's least expensive and easiest to work with is nylon sheet stock about $\frac{3}{32}$ inch thick. It is stiff enough to hold its shape but flexible enough to move with the rudder. Moreover, you can easily fair the leading and trailing edges to make a smooth transition from gelcoat to plastic fairing strip. The strip should just cover the gap between the rudder and the skeg even when the rudder is turned. The trailing edge of the fairing strip will rub gently against the radiused forward edge of the rudder. You won't be able to measure the improvement in your boat's performance resulting from adding these fairing strips by looking at your knotmeter, but it's the kind of incremental change that can make the difference between winning and losing in a tight race.

Rudder fairing strips

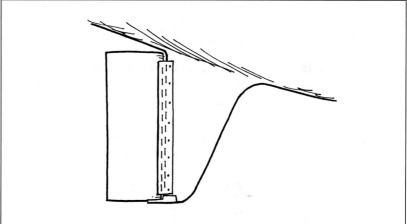

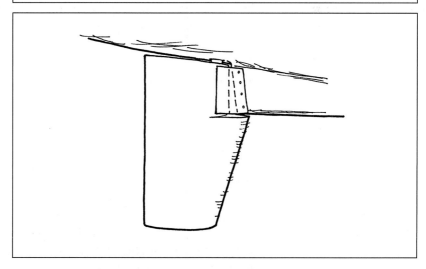

FEATHERING PROPELLERS

The most dramatic single thing you can do below the waterline to increase boat speed is to replace your fixed-blade propeller with a feathering or folding prop. Each has advantages and disadvantages, and there are a variety of designs for each on the market. Among feathering props, my interest is piqued by four different products. I should note, however, that the knot of boat speed gained by changing to one of these propellers comes at a cost. They are more pricey compared with the propellers they replace because the blades pivot so that even in reverse the designed leading edges of the blade are always cutting the water. For example, the list price of a 14-inch-diameter three-blade feathering propeller for a 1- to 1¼-inch shaft is about $2,000—a little less for some props, a bit more for others. A comparable fixed-blade prop costs only about $350. Similarly, the list price for a 21-inch three-blade feathering propeller for a 1½-inch shaft is between $3,000 and $3,500, but a comparable fixed-blade propeller is about $600.

Max-Prop. The Max-Prop is probably the most widely used feathering propeller among cruising sailors at least in part because it was the first to be widely promoted. The design of the Max-Prop results in a propeller with very low drag—good for boosting performance under sail—but only moderate efficiency when moving forward under power because of its relatively large hub and the inefficiency of its flat, ear-shaped blades. Like other feathering propellers, however, it provides better performance in reverse than does a fixed-blade propeller. Although the pitch of traditional Max-Props can be changed only when the boat is out of the water, the company has introduced a newer model, the Max-Prop VP (Variable Pitch), which has a patented system for adjusting the propeller's pitch while the boat is in the water without need for any tools. The in-the-water pitch-adjustment feature is available at this writing only on three-blade props for shafts with a diameter of 1¼ to 2 inches. Depending upon propeller size, the VP models cost from $400 to $1,300, more than the usual Max-Prop.

J-Prop. The most appealing feature of Bomon's J-Prop feathering propeller is the ease of changing the propeller's pitch, even underwater. This is accomplished by pulling out a spring-loaded nose hub and rotating the hub clockwise or counterclockwise to increase or decrease the pitch, then letting the hub reseat itself. In other respects the J-Prop is similar to other conventional feathering props. It creates very little drag when feathered, but its flat blades make it less effective than a fixed-blade propeller when going forward under power. As is characteristic of feathering propellers, however, its performance in reverse is notably better than that of a comparable fixed-blade propeller. The J-Prop is available in two- or three-blade models.

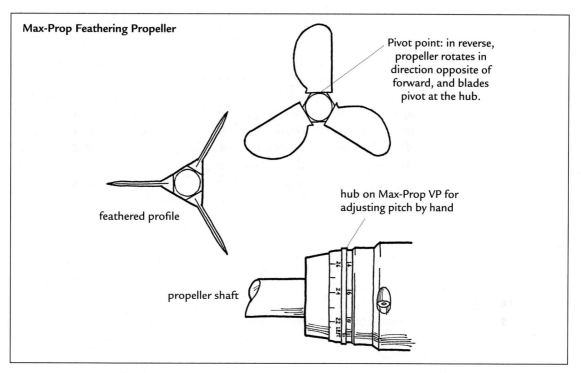

Max-Prop Feathering Propeller

Pivot point: in reverse, propeller rotates in direction opposite of forward, and blades pivot at the hub.

feathered profile

hub on Max-Prop VP for adjusting pitch by hand

propeller shaft

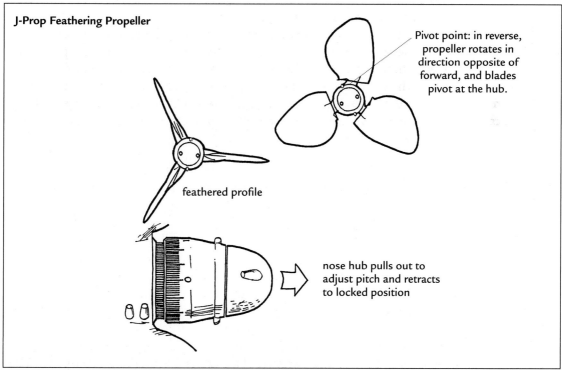

J-Prop Feathering Propeller

Pivot point: in reverse, propeller rotates in direction opposite of forward, and blades pivot at the hub.

feathered profile

nose hub pulls out to adjust pitch and retracts to locked position

Feathering propellers

Autoprop. This European import has the most unusual design among the feathering props. However, it is a very efficient variable-pitch propeller. Under power, the pitch of the propeller's three blades adjusts automatically with changes in engine speed and boat speed through the water to provide maximum thrust at all times. In addition, it provides good performance in reverse, particularly if you need to stop in a hurry. Depending upon your individual needs, the possible downsides to the Autoprop are that its unique design creates slightly more drag than some of the more "conventional" feathering propellers and that it may require a prop lock because of its tendency to rotate when you're sailing at higher speeds.

Luke. The name Paul Luke is probably best known among cruising sailors for the Luke three-piece storm anchor. However, the P. E. Luke Company has also been manufacturing and selling three-blade feathering propellers since the 1960s. Two features set the Luke feathering propeller apart: its blades are shaped using a helical twist that provides for uniform thrust across the whole blade, resulting in a more powerful propeller; and its design allows it to fit in the same space occupied by an existing fixed-blade propeller without shortening the shaft (most feathering propellers project beyond the end of the prop shaft). As a result, the Luke feathering propeller can be used in full-keel boats whose propeller aperture will not accommodate other feathering props. One limitation to the Luke propeller is that its pitch can only be adjusted at the factory. The Luke propeller also has a larger hub and therefore creates slightly more drag than other feathering props, making it better suited for larger boats whose thicker keels make the hub diameter a moot point.

FOLDING PROPELLERS

The alternative to a feathering propeller is one whose blades fold up when not in use. In fact, folding propellers have been the propeller of choice for racing sailors for many years because of their exceptionally low drag. When the blades are folded—as they would be under sail—folding propellers also are effectively snagproof. That is, you don't have to worry about anything fouling your propeller while you are under sail.

Despite these advantages, however, most cruising sailors have been reluctant to use folding props for at least three reasons: it is sometimes difficult to get folding props to open unless the boat is stopped dead in the water; folding props have developed a reputation for being unreliable in reverse; and early folding props designs had a problem with only one blade opening, throwing the propeller and shaft

Autoprop Variable-Pitch Feathering Propeller

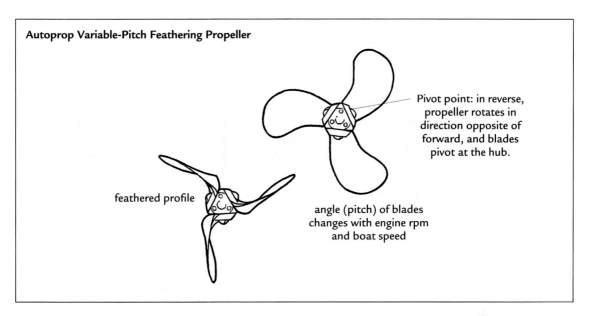

Pivot point: in reverse, propeller rotates in direction opposite of forward, and blades pivot at the hub.

feathered profile

angle (pitch) of blades changes with engine rpm and boat speed

Luke Feathering Propeller

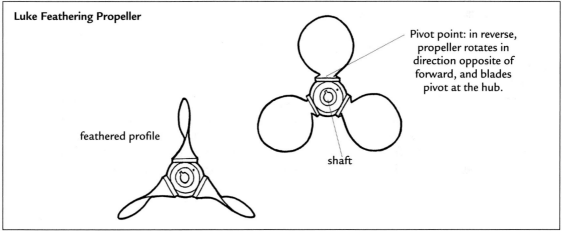

Pivot point: in reverse, propeller rotates in direction opposite of forward, and blades pivot at the hub.

feathered profile

shaft

Flex-O-Fold Folding Propeller

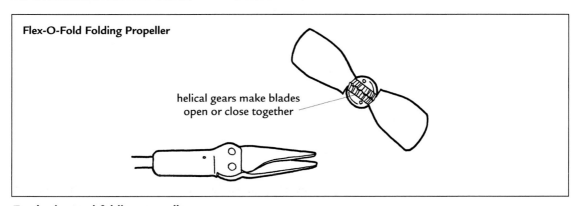

helical gears make blades open or close together

Feathering and folding propellers

badly out of balance and potentially damaging the boat or the transmission.

Newer designs have attacked these problems, and the Flex-O-Fold propeller (see page 125) comes the closest I've seen to addressing all three effectively. First, the Flex-O-Fold propeller's blades are geared to one another so that all must open together. Second, the cruising version of the propeller—yes, there are separate cruising and racing versions of the same propeller—is designed so that there is a gap between the blades when they are folded to make them easier to open. Third, the outer edges of each blade overlap the adjacent blades near the tip when folded so that those overlapping edges will "grab" the water when the propeller begins to turn, forcing the blades open. Fourth, the blades have been made heavier so that there is added centrifugal force to help them open. And finally, the blades have been designed with an airfoil shape to provide greater—and impressive—thrust.

Even with all of these improvements, however, there remains one possible downside to the Flex-O-Fold propeller that is inherent in the basic concept of folding propellers: Water flowing past the prop as a boat coasts forward will close the blades when the transmission is shifted from forward into neutral and will tend to keep the blades closed as the gears go into reverse. Moreover, the faster the boat is moving through the water, the more likely this problem is to arise. The question is whether you could stop the boat in a hurry if you had to. This is one of those cases in which it would be a good idea to go for a demonstration run before making a purchase to be satisfied that the blade will open reliably in reverse in the conditions you expect to encounter. It may well be that for long-distance cruising, when one spends little time trying to maneuver in tight quarters in a marina, this folding propeller will suit your needs. List prices of the Flex-O-Fold two- and three-blade folding propellers are comparable to those of feathering props.

ABOVE THE WATERLINE

Once you move above the waterline, you have a whole series of options.

BOOM VANG

Adding a boom vang to your boat will enhance your ability to adjust the sail shape for optimum sailing efficiency. You should consult with a rigger about the design and specifications of a vang for your specific boat; however, one excellent design begins with a curved stainless steel plate shaped to fit a bit more than halfway around the mast. A sturdy fin with a hole to receive a shackle is welded to this plate, which is then secured to the mast near deck level using machine screws. The mast is drilled and tapped to receive the machine screws. A thin piece of neoprene, polyethylene, or flexible nylon sheeting will serve as a barrier between the stainless steel plate and the aluminum mast to prevent galvanic corrosion. Dip the machine screws in silicone before screwing them into the mast for the same reason. The boom end of the vang is secured to one or more bails bolted to the boom using compression tubes. The cost of a well-rigged block-and-tackle boom vang on a 35-foot boat, including the mast bracket and boom bails, is from $500 to $800.

Boom vang

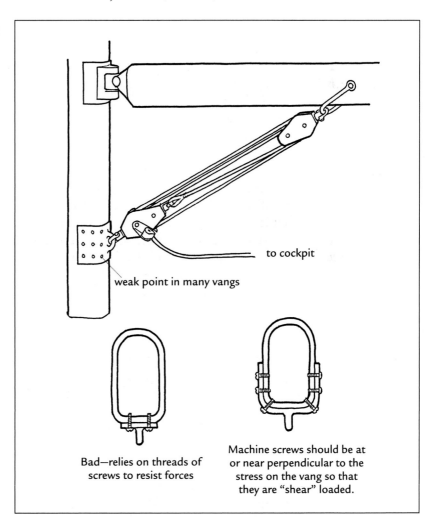

to cockpit

weak point in many vangs

Bad—relies on threads of screws to resist forces

Machine screws should be at or near perpendicular to the stress on the vang so that they are "shear" loaded.

FULL-BATTEN MAINSAIL

Many if not most boats that take part in major ocean races use full-batten mainsails. And there's a reason. A full-batten mainsail with a maximum-roach sail provides more sail area and requires considerably less work to optimize performance because the sail shape is set by the battens. A full-batten mainsail will almost certainly improve your boat's performance on all points of sail.

An existing mainsail in good condition can be converted to a full-batten sail for somewhere between $400 and $1,000. For inshore and coastal cruising a sail using your mast's existing track will be adequate. For offshore cruising you should have an external track installed—an additional $1,000 to $3,000. The reason is that while the slides of a traditional mainsail are in tension and the sail can be pulled down (e.g., for reefing) even when the sail is drawing, the cars of a full-batten mainsail are in compression, actually being pushed hard against the mast. If those cars are mounted on normal mainsail tracks, the sail cannot be pulled down for reefing unless the load is taken off the cars by luffing the main—not necessarily what you want to be doing in building winds and seas offshore.

Using one of the two kinds of external track recommended—a track designed for use with ball-bearing cars (similar to the familiar Harken genoa track system) or the Antal track and batcar system—the sail can be pulled down while under load. Both systems can be installed without unstepping your mast. Of the two, the Antal system is the less expensive.

CRUISING SPINNAKER WITH A SOCK

A cruising spinnaker can make a huge difference in your boat's performance off the wind in light to moderate air. Moreover, the addition of an effective sock system for rigging and dousing the chute makes the spinnaker user-friendly for shorthanded crews. If sailing coastwise or in the Bahamas, have your spinnaker made of ¾-ounce nylon. If cruising in windier regions or for rail-down reaching, consider having your sail made of 1½-ounce nylon. The heavier fabric will last three to four times as long as the lighter cloth. However, you do need to consider how much your cruising spinnaker and sock will weigh in the sailbag and how large that sailbag will be when deciding what weight cloth to use. As we learned the hard way, a large chute made of 1½-ounce fabric can make a pretty hefty and bulky load to wrestle up to the foredeck. The cost of a cruising spinnaker and sock will be between $1,000 and $3,000 for boats in the 28- to 45-foot range.

Full-batten mainsail

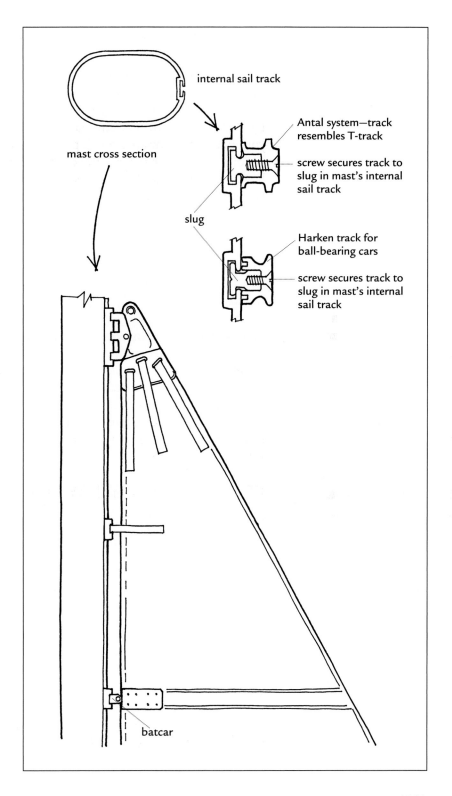

internal sail track

Antal system—track
resembles T-track

screw secures track to
slug in mast's internal
sail track

mast cross section

slug

Harken track for
ball-bearing cars

screw secures track to
slug in mast's internal
sail track

batcar

Hints for using your cruising spinnaker: Set the chute while sailing on a reach so that it can't twist coming out of the sock. Then, fall off downwind if that's where you want to go. To retrieve the chute, push the boat all the way off the wind and let out enough on the sheet to spill wind from the sail. The sock cannot be pulled down over a chute that's filled hard with wind. Finally, do not try to flatten the sail by taking in on the tack pendant when you're reaching. Because of the way cruising spinnakers are cut, tightening the tack pendant will have the opposite effect, making the chute fuller and therefore less effective.

TANDEM HEADSAILS

Installing a second stay just aft of your present headstay lets you rig two different headsails with roller-furling gear. If you already have an inner forestay for a staysail, you can move the bottom of that inner forestay forward substantially. A good distance between the tacks of the two headsails is 18 inches, but they can be separated by as much as 24 to 30 inches. The two stays need not be parallel—and they obviously will not be parallel if you are moving the inner forestay forward.

Tandem headsails

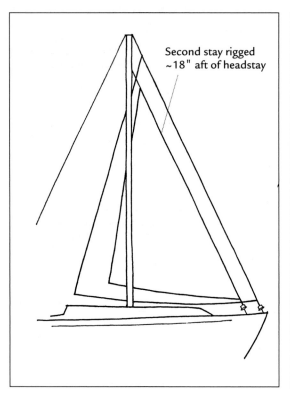

Second stay rigged ~18" aft of headstay

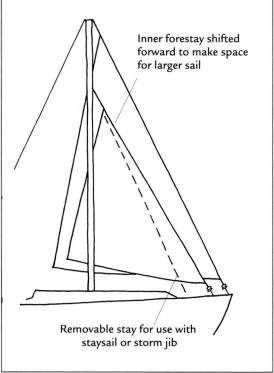

Inner forestay shifted forward to make space for larger sail

Removable stay for use with staysail or storm jib

The advantage of this system is that you have in reality two head-sails to work with rather than a headsail and a staysail. As a result, you can put a large roller-furling genoa on your headstay to improve your light-air performance and a roller-furling sail that is significantly larger than the usual staysail on the second stay. Additionally, the inner headsail can be designed for roller reefing for use in stronger winds. A third removable stay added where your old staysail was secured can serve as the backup for a storm jib; the removable stay can be stowed at the shrouds when not in use, see illustrations on pages 46 and 47.

TRIMMING THE JIB

Most cruising sailors don't adjust their jibsheet leads very often. The reason is simple: it's too much work to clip on to the jack lines, get out of the cockpit, and then try to move the genoa car on its track. As a result, cruising sailors often do not get the best performance from their headsails. The obvious answer is to take a lesson from racing sailors and install a system for adjusting your jibsheet leads from the cockpit—a system so easy to use that you can't resist tweaking the set of your jib.

Adjusting the genoa lead from the cockpit

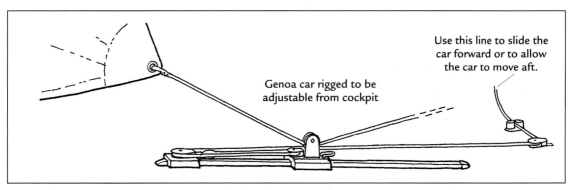

Use this line to slide the car forward or to allow the car to move aft.

Genoa car rigged to be adjustable from cockpit

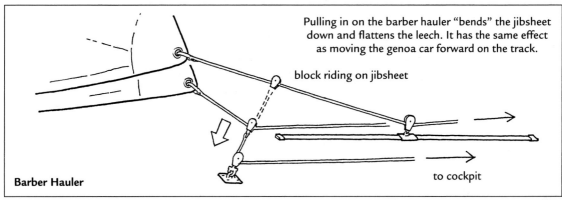

Pulling in on the barber hauler "bends" the jibsheet down and flattens the leech. It has the same effect as moving the genoa car forward on the track.

block riding on jibsheet

Barber Hauler

to cockpit

There are three approaches to choose from. The first, and most expensive, is to install a Harken track and ball-bearing genoa car system rigged so that the car can be adjusted even under load from the cockpit. The second is to use the Antal genoa car made with a "self lubricating" composite lining that allows the car to slide under load on a conventional T-track and rig this system so that it can be adjusted from the cockpit. This car uses the same lining that's in the Antal cars for full-batten mainsails.

The third and least expensive approach is to rig a "barber hauler." This consists of two separate blocks, each with a length of rope attached to it. Each block is threaded onto a jibsheet so that the sheet runs freely through the block. The lines tied to those blocks run through turning blocks attached on deck somewhere between the midship cleat and the shrouds and then run back to the cockpit. The turning blocks can be rigged to a midship cleat, a deck-mounted padeye secured with a backing plate, the toe rail, the ear of a stanchion base, or even to the chainplate for the aft lower shroud. In use, the jibsheet lead is adjusted by pulling in or easing the barber hauler, the line to the block on your jibsheet. When you pull in on the barber hauler, the jibsheet is bent down toward the deck, tightening the leech and flattening the sail. Easing the barber hauler lets the sail resume its fuller shape.

6

MAKE YOUR BOAT
Look Better

*W*e've all had the experience of walking along a dock and being stopped dead in our tracks by a particularly impressive boat. It may be a mean, lean racing machine. It may have the appearance of a world cruiser. Or it may have the look of something clearly defined between those two extremes. But whatever it is, you know the purpose of this boat just by looking at it. And you can enjoy just looking at it, admiring the way it all fits together. That's what we're after.

My focus here is not pure cosmetics—paint, gelcoat, brightwork, metal surfaces, canvas work—or making sure that everything is clean and beautiful. I assume that you know all about that. I'm interested in changes you can make to your cruising boat in addition to those suggested in earlier chapters that will help make your boat look more like the cruising boat you want it to be. That is, changes that will help your boat's appearance more closely define its function and distinguish it from the many boats similar to it.

Most of my suggestions are relatively modest—all but two, in fact. But all will result in distinctive changes to the appearance of your boat—changes that will dress up your boat, changes that will make it look saltier, and changes that will make it look more substantial. But all are functional, form defining function.

DRESSING UP YOUR BOAT

There is nothing like a little bit of teak, a little less gelcoat, or something a little out of the ordinary to dress up your boat. If, at the same time, the dressing can serve a real purpose, that's even better.

133

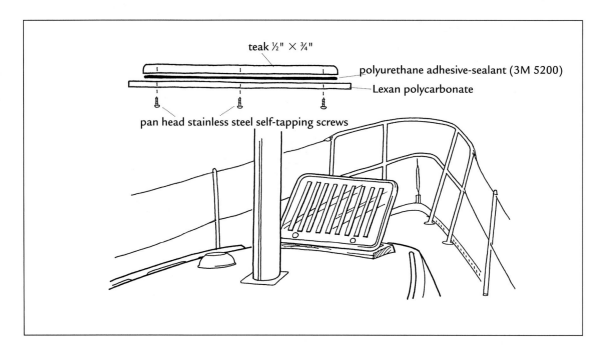

teak ½" × ¾"

polyurethane adhesive-sealant (3M 5200)

Lexan polycarbonate

pan head stainless steel self-tapping screws

Teak nonskid for deck hatches

DECK HATCHES

Installing strips of teak ¾ inch wide and ½ inch thick spaced about 2 inches apart on the Lexan polycarbonate "window" in deck hatches larger than about 12 inches square will do double duty. It will add a nonskid surface to your deck hatches and help break up the plastic look. Use three or four #6 pan head self-tapping screws from the underside of the hatch to attach each strip and brown polyurethane adhesive-sealant to glue them in place and seal against leaks. When installing the strips, tighten the screws by hand, being careful not to overtighten them. It's important not to squeeze all of the adhesive-sealant out from under the teak strips. Use a %₄-inch bit to drill holes in the Lexan and a ¹⁄₁₆-inch bit to drill a starter hole (¼ in. deep) in the teak. (Any time you make a hole in Lexan for a screw or bolt, the hole should be a little bit larger than the fastener to allow for thermal expansion and contraction of the Lexan.) The length of your screw should be equal to the thickness of the Lexan plus ¼ inch. Allow a week for the adhesive-sealant to cure before stepping on the teak strips, longer in cold weather.

DORADE BOXES

Replacing the teak or fiberglass tops of your Dorade boxes with ⅜-inch Lexan will not only dress up your Dorades (adding a touch of modernity to traditional teak Dorades or a break from gelcoat in

Lexan top for Dorade box

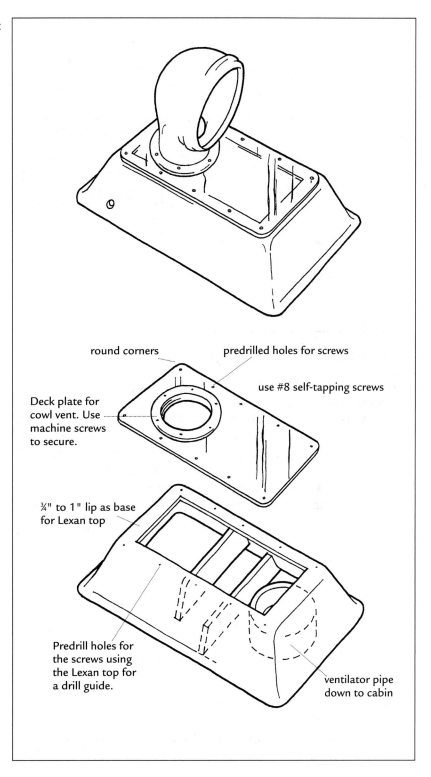

round corners

predrilled holes for screws

Deck plate for cowl vent. Use machine screws to secure.

use #8 self-tapping screws

¾" to 1" lip as base for Lexan top

Predrill holes for the screws using the Lexan top for a drill guide.

ventilator pipe down to cabin

fiberglass Dorades) but also turn your ventilator into a small overhead window from the cabin below. When cutting out the top of your fiberglass or wood Dorade box, be sure to leave a ¾- to 1-inch lip around the edge of the box to serve as a base for your new Lexan top. You will have to use a hole saw to cut the Lexan to receive the deck plate for the cowl vent. A drill press will make cutting the hole much easier. When drilling or sawing Lexan, avoid prolonged cuts so that the saw blade and drill bit do not get hot. Bed the Lexan with polyurethane adhesive-sealant along the lip of the Dorade box. Use self-tapping screws to secure the Lexan top to your Dorade box, tightening the screws by hand to avoid overtightening them and squeezing out the sealant.

FENDERBOARD-GANGWAY

If you have a 6-foot or longer stretch of space about 1 foot wide inside the handrails on your cabintop, you can rig an attractive fenderboard that will do double duty as a gangway for those times when a little help getting from the boat to the dock would be welcome. The two keys to making this work are finding a good looking 2-by-10-inch board of the length you want and installing a set of chocks on

Fenderboard-gangway

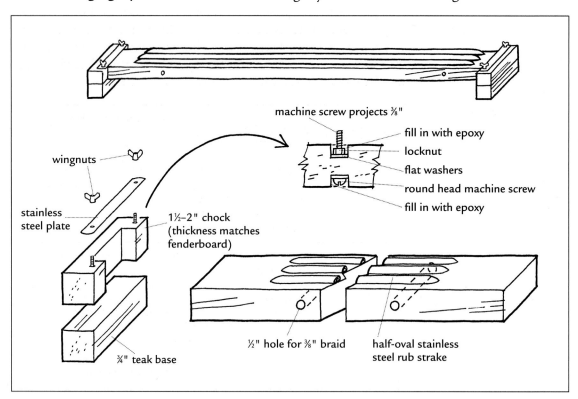

machine screw projects ⅜"

fill in with epoxy

locknut

flat washers

round head machine screw

fill in with epoxy

wingnuts

stainless steel plate

1½–2" chock (thickness matches fenderboard)

½" hole for ⅜" braid

half-oval stainless steel rub strake

¾" teak base

the cabintop for stowing the board. With the board in hand, you can either paint it or finish it as you would teak and install a series of four half-oval stainless steel rub strakes on one side of the board, running almost its full length. Then, using a long, ½-inch auger bit, drill a hole through the width of the board about 1 foot from each end. When you're going to use the fenderboard-gangway, feed a length of ⅜-inch braided line through each of the holes either to hang your fenderboard alongside or to secure the ends of your gangway. When the board is not in use, stow it in chocks on the cabintop.

TEAK WINDOW FRAMES

If your boat has Lexan windows secured directly to the fiberglass cabinhouse, you will be amazed at how installing teak window frames will enhance your boat's appearance. The frames serve two purposes, especially if your windows need replacing because of age. They diffuse the stresses caused by uneven tightening of the bolts securing the windows, making them less likely to crack around the bolts, and they help protect against leaks.

Unless your windows are mounted flush with the cabinhouse, making the window frames will not be easy and is probably best left to a good ship's carpenter. Whether or not your windows are flush-mounted, the frames should be made to fit around the circumference of the windows, overlapping the window by at least 1 inch, more if needed to allow for the bolt heads. Upon installation, bed the frames and the windows well with a silicone or acrylic sealant.

Teak window frames

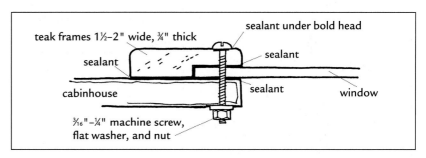

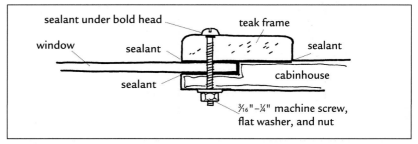

MAKING YOUR BOAT SALTIER

The suggestions for making your boat saltier speak to how you use your boat and your ability to meet your needs while cruising.

FISHING ROD HOLDERS

Fishing under sail sounds easy enough, but to one who has fished while sailing without rod holders, these make a lot of sense. They also look purposeful. So if you sail where trolling a line astern might result in catching your dinner, rod holders port and starboard on the stern rail or on the first stanchion forward from the stern rail will make fishing easier. Just drop your lure astern, put your fishing rod in the leeward rod holder, set the ratchet and drag, and wait for the action.

PINRAILS

Teak pinrails port and starboard in your lower shrouds, each holding four or five belaying pins, not only look salty but also provide a handy place to tie off halyards, secure flag and radar reflector halyards, and stow spare lines. They are also easy to make if you have access to a table saw and a wood lathe. If a lathe is not available, you can make the belaying pins round with sandpaper and patience.

The easiest way to make pinrails is to use ¼ stock that is a full 4 inches wide, that is, lumber with a finished thickness of 1 full inch. Locate the pinrails about waist high when you are standing next to the mast. Measure the distance between the lower shrouds at that height and add 6 inches. Cut four pieces of teak to that length, then trim each of the pieces to a 3-inch width. Set the trimmings aside; you'll make them into your belaying pins later.

Using C-clamps, fasten one piece of your pinrail to the shrouds at the desired height. Mark that height by wrapping black electrical tape around the shrouds just under the piece of teak. Position the wood so that it extends the same distance beyond the two shrouds (about 2 in. at the bottom) and secure the clamps just tight enough to hold the wood in place (but not so tight as to distort the wire). Carefully scribe the lines formed on the teak by the inside and outside edges of the shrouds. Also, carefully measure the thickness of the shrouds. After removing the board, cut a groove between the angled lines you've drawn for the shrouds near each end of the board. The depth of that groove should be equal to the thickness of the shroud. Experiment on a scrap of wood to adjust the height of your table saw blade and practice making the cut a few times. Keep in

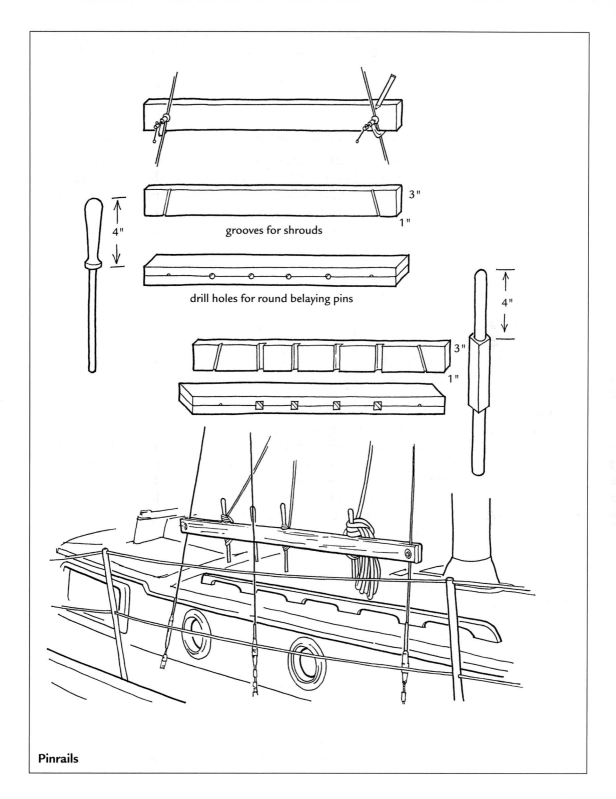

grooves for shrouds

3"

1"

4"

drill holes for round belaying pins

3"

1"

4"

Pinrails

mind that it is better to make the groove a bit too narrow and shallow than to make it too big. You can always use a round file or sandpaper to enlarge the groove if it is too small.

Once you've repeated this process on a second board for the other set of shrouds, the most challenging work is completed. Each pinrail consists of two of the 3-inch boards, one notched to fit over the shrouds, the other screwed to the first board to enclose the shrouds in their grooves. The result is a pinrail that is 2 inches thick and 3 inches wide (vertically).

Now you're ready to make the belaying pins. Each pin should be about 10 inches long, so cut the roughly 1-inch-square strips that you trimmed from the original boards into 10-inch lengths. Using a lathe, you can turn those square 10-inch pegs into round pins ¾ to ⅞ inch thick, making little flanges on the pins about 4 inches from one end (that end will be the top). Keep in mind that you will need to drill holes in the pinrail to receive the round pins; this means that the pins must be the same thickness as your drill bit. Either an auger bit or a speed bit will serve to drill the holes, though an auger bit will probably make a neater hole.

If you don't have access to a lathe, you'll have to use a different approach. First, using your table saw, trim the strips so that they are the same thickness in both directions—that is, so that they have a square cross section. Next, after cutting the strips into 10-inch lengths, disassemble the pinrails, open them wide as you would a hot-dog roll, lay the "square" pins across the two halves of the pinrail exactly where you want them in the finished rail—about 6 inches apart—and draw lines to show both sides of each rail. Then measure the thickness of the square rails and remove half of that amount from between the lines on each of the pinrail halves. Practice using two scraps of lumber until you have the saw blade adjusted precisely. The square pins should fit snugly in the cutout when the two halves of the rail are refastened.

When all of the pinrails have been notched to receive the square pins, you can use sandpaper to make the top and bottom portions of the pins round. The 3 inches of each pin that will be enclosed in the pinrail should remain square. Preassemble the pinrail and the pins on your workbench using 1½-inch #8 stainless steel self-tapping screws, predrilling ¹⁄₁₆-inch guide holes for the screws. In addition to the screws holding the pinrails together, use one screw from each side to secure each of the pins.

To install the pinrails on the shrouds, remove one side of each rail (leaving the pins in place in the other side) and assemble the rails on the shrouds. You don't need to worry about the rails sliding up or down on the shrouds. The geometry of the shrouds should prevent that. As a final step, you can round off all corners and hard edges with sandpaper and finish them the same way you finish your other exterior teak. Note: do not glue the pinrail assembly together—you may need to remove it some day.

V-BERTH WORKBENCH

Instead of using your chart table, galley counters, or a cockpit seat when you need workbench space, wouldn't it be nice to have an actual workbench in the forward cabin under the side deck that can be opened up for use? When the workbench is "closed," it forms a vertical wall along the outboard edge of the berth up to the side deck above.

The bench portion of the workbench consists of a piece of ¾-inch plywood hinged at the bottom so that it opens down onto the berth. Either cover the outside of the plywood (the side that shows when the bench is folded up) with a plastic laminate such as Formica trimmed along the edges with teak or use a veneered plywood for your workbench. A piece of stainless steel sheet stock covers the work surface. Shelves equipped with deep fiddles form bins that fill the space between the hull (liner) and the closed bench. These bins can be used to stow tools, fasteners, and so on. This workbench is especially handy if your V-berth has a cutout in the middle so that you can stand in front of the open bench while using it.

V-berth workbench

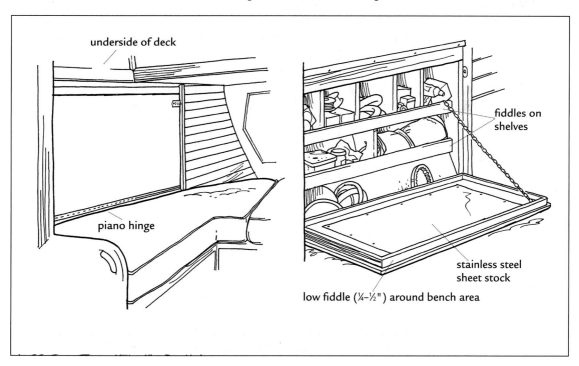

underside of deck

piano hinge

fiddles on shelves

stainless steel sheet stock

low fiddle (¼–½") around bench area

MAKING YOUR BOAT LOOK MORE SUBSTANTIAL

Cruising boats are used differently than racers or daysailers. They often go into strange marinas. They tend to use their anchors more. In fact, the whole boat gets used more and can suffer cosmetically from use. As a result, cruising sailors are often more concerned than others with building in components designed to protect their boats from the heavy use they receive. And those protective components make a boat more substantial not only in appearance but in fact.

PROTECTING THE ANCHOR CHAIN AGAINST CHAFING

Nothing will scar a foredeck faster than dragging anchor chain across it or letting an anchor shank wear on it. A protective strip between your bow-roller assembly and your windlass, anchor locker hatch or chain pipe in the anchor locker will prevent such damage. The protective strip can be a teak board ¾ inch thick or a sheet of stainless steel shaped to fit the contour of your deck. If you use stainless steel, have the sheet installed professionally unless you have the special skills and tools needed. The teak or stainless steel should be bedded well with a sealant and can be secured with self-tapping screws, countersunk to provide a smooth surface.

Protecting the foredeck

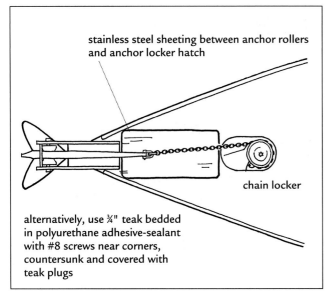

stainless steel sheeting between anchor rollers and anchor locker hatch

chain locker

alternatively, use ¾" teak bedded in polyurethane adhesive-sealant with #8 screws near corners, countersunk and covered with teak plugs

BOW AND STEM SHIELDS

Anchor flukes can chip away at a boat's stem when the anchor knocks against the bow as the crew brings it up. This kind of damage can be prevented by installing a stainless steel shield along the stem. It may only be necessary to protect a few inches of the stem on each side, though I've seen boats with much larger stem shields. Similarly, if your anchor in its bow roller tends to rub against the hull, a piece of stainless steel sheet stock over that part of the bow will further protect your hull. Finally, if you pull your anchor up at a

Bow and stem shields

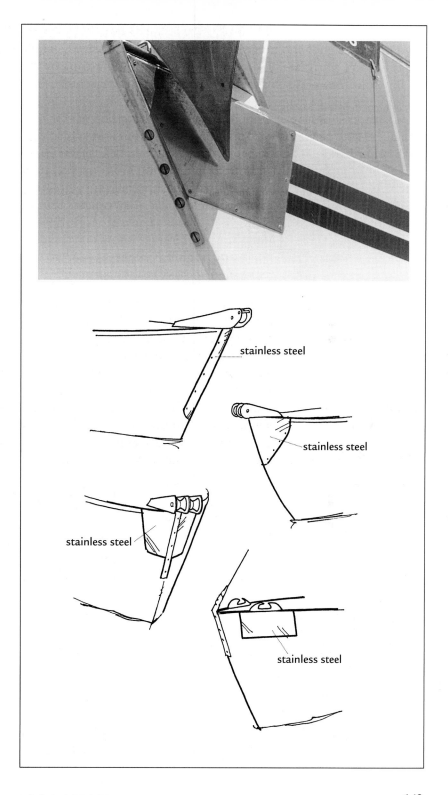

stainless steel

stainless steel

stainless steel

stainless steel

chock near the bow, stainless steel sheeting to protect the hull below the bow chocks port and starboard may be in order.

PROTECTION AGAINST CHAFE

Wherever a line runs across teak or over a fiberglass edge—even across the cabinhouse—install half-oval stainless steel rub strakes to protect the teak or gelcoat from chafe. The rub strakes are available from most major marine stores in a variety of lengths ranging from 8 to 24 inches. Bed the rub strakes well with silicone.

PROTECTING DECK VENTILATORS

Anytime a cowl vent protrudes from the deck, it's a potential line snagger. Not only can that foul up a line but it can cost you a ventilator if a jibsheet fouls it and the jib fills suddenly, yanking hard on the fouled sheet. Three-legged stainless steel ventilator guardrails

Ventilator guardrails

will not only dress up the deck but also provide effective protection for your ventilators and help keep your sheets running freely. They will even prove handy for tying off a line or two.

RUBRAILS

Most fiberglass sailboats are constructed without the benefit of rubrails. For racing, that's OK. For a cruising boat, however, a rubrail is close to a necessity. Moreover, if your boat does not have a rubrail, adding one will change its appearance dramatically. It will also let you breathe a little easier the next time you come into a strange slip in difficult currents and bump against a piling.

Admittedly, adding a rubrail to your boat is a major project. It is not terribly difficult, however. It requires mostly time and patience. It's also much easier if you have a second pair of hands available.

There are two ways to approach this project: either use multiple layers of teak to build a wood rubrail, securing it with screws and polyurethane adhesive-sealant or install a single-thickness preshaped teak rubrail, possibly using machine screws to bolt portions of it to the hull, bedding it with the adhesive-sealant. In general, the rubrail should run from the stern as far forward as it will be effective. At some point the flare of the bow may make extending the rubrail farther forward unnecessary or difficult because of the need to twist the wood to fit the flare.

From a practical viewpoint, fabricating a rubrail from two or, preferably, three relatively thin layers of wood is the easier approach. Ideally, the rubrail will project about 1½ inches from the hull. You'll need teak boards 3 inches wide and ½ inch thick and, depending upon the size of your boat, either a ¾-inch or a 1-inch stainless steel half-oval rubrail that is drilled and countersunk for screws every 6 inches. You'll also need a lot of brown polyurethane adhesive-sealant and a lot of #12 stainless steel pan head self-tapping screws and flat washers. The screws will be in three lengths (assuming there are three layers of wood in the rubrail). The first set of screws should be long enough to penetrate the first layer of wood and the hull laminate; the second set should be ½ inch longer (assuming the wood is ½ in. thick), and the third set should be ½ inch longer still. The goal is for the screws in all three layers of the rubrail to penetrate the hull laminate.

If you must join two or more boards to get the length you want, be sure that the overlapping ends are pointed aft and make your joint along the flat portion of the run. You may prefer to shape the boards before installing them. Most people like the rubrail to be wide where

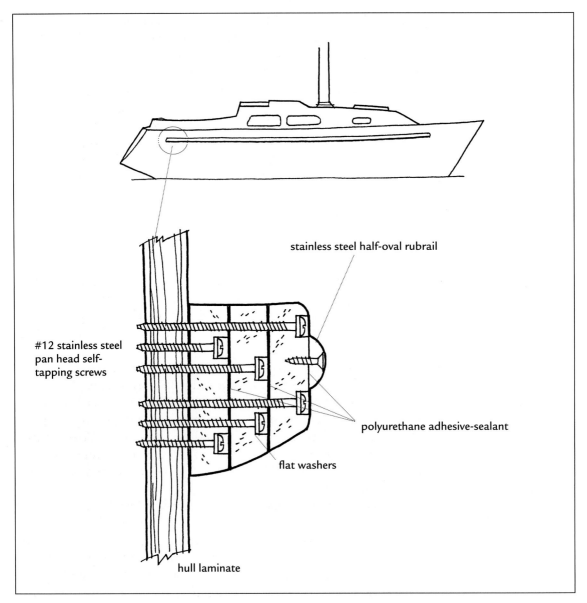

stainless steel half-oval rubrail

#12 stainless steel pan head self-tapping screws

polyurethane adhesive-sealant

flat washers

hull laminate

Adding rubrails

it meets the hull, somewhat narrower at the outside, more or less flat on the top, and angled down toward the hull on the bottom. To begin, hold the first board in place and mark it where you want to put each pair of screws (top and bottom) along the length of the board. In general, the screw pairs should be about 9 inches apart, possibly closer around curves.

Next, predrill screw holes in the wood, countersinking the holes just enough that the screw heads with their flat washers will be flush with the board surface. Then, holding the board in position and using the holes in the wood as guides, drill the first holes in the hull, starting at the middle of the board. Insert the first screws with their flat washers and tighten them firmly, but do not overtighten them. (You'll need to take them out and put them back in later.) Then drill holes for the screws that will be 18 inches away in both directions (i.e., skip a pair of holes in each direction) and drive those screws. These six screws should hold the board securely while you work your way along the board in both directions drilling all of the holes in the hull and inserting screws as needed to make the board hug the hull.

When all the holes for mounting the first board have been drilled, remove the board and apply a uniform but thin coating of polyurethane adhesive-sealant (brown) to the back of the board. Insert the original six screws (around the middle) so that they stick out a small amount and mount the board once again. This time, tighten the screws until they begin squeezing out the polyurethane adhesive-sealant. Continue fastening the board in place, working from the middle to the ends. Repeat this process until the first layer of teak is mounted for both rubrails.

Before starting on the second layer of teak, mark the location of each pair of screws on the top edge of the first layer. Then, following the same procedure as before, add the second layer of teak, bedding it with polyurethane adhesive-sealant and screws long enough to penetrate both the first layer of teak and the hull laminate. These screws also should be spaced every 9 inches, offset 3 inches from the screws securing the first layer. Mark the position of these new screws on the top edge of the rail.

Add the third and final layer of teak following the same procedure but countersinking the screw heads an additional ⅛ inch below the wood surface so that you can cover them later with teak plugs. If there is a significant bend or twist along any section of your rubrail, wait a few days after finishing one layer of teak before installing the next layer to give the polyurethane adhesive-sealant a chance to cure so that not all of the stress will be on the screws. When you have installed all the layers of teak and shaped the rail as desired, glue the teak plugs over the screw heads, sand them down, and apply the half-oval stainless steel rub strake along the full length of your rubrail.

If you want to build your rubrail using a single thickness of teak, you will be somewhat limited in how much you can bend the board to follow the curvature of your hull. The fact is that a board thicker than 1 inch may be difficult, though not necessarily impossible, to bend around the curve of the hull, so that you risk splitting a piece of rather expensive lumber. Moreover, if much bending is required, you'll need access to the inside of the hull so that you can bolt parts of the board to the hull using ¼-inch round head machine screws with fender washers as miniature backing plates and locknuts. If, however, the run for the rail is effectively flat with little bending required, and if you have ½ inch or more of solid fiberglass behind your rubrail, you can probably make the installation using #12 screws, with flat washers under their heads to keep them from digging into the wood. Using polyurethane adhesive-sealant as a bedding compound will also help secure the rubrail to the hull once it has cured.

MARINE VENDORS

Most of the vendors listed here have sales offices and/or distributors in many countries around the world. To find the office nearest you, go to the company's website or request information by e-mail. Otherwise, products can be purchased directly from the vendor.

ANCHOR WINDLASS

Lewmar Marine
351 New Whitfield St.
Guilford CT 06437
203-458-6200
www.lewmar.com

Simpson Lawrence USA, Inc.
6208 28th St. E.
Bradenton FL 34203-4123
800-946-3527
E-mail: info@simpson-lawrence-usa.com
www.slengineering.com

BOATING PUBLICATIONS

Practical Sailor
14 Regatta Way
Portsmouth RI 02871
E-mail: PSBelvoir@aol.com
Subscriptions: P.O. Box 420235
Palm Coast FL 32142-0235
800-829-9087

Sailboat Buyers Guide (to sailboats and gear),
published annually by *SAIL* magazine
84 State St.
Boston MA 02109-2202
617-720-8600

DUTCHMAN BOOM BRAKE

Dutchman—Martinus Van Breems, Inc.
160 Water St.
Norwalk CT 06854
203-838-0375
E-mail: dutchman@sailnet.com
www.dutchmanproducts.com

FLUORESCENT CABIN LIGHTS

Alpen Glow
P.O. Box 415
Eureka MT 59917
406-889-3586

FUEL-CLEANING SYSTEMS

DeBug—Environmental Solutions International, Inc.
11002 Racoon Ridge
Reston VA 20191-4911
800-411-3284
E-mail: info@DE-BUG.com
www.de-bug.com

PuraTec—IPS, Inc.
P.O. Box 1333
Newport RI 02840
800-323-5868
E-mail: IPSworld@netscape.net
www.IPSworld.com

IMS RACING CERTIFICATES

US Sailing
P.O. Box 1260
15 Maritime Dr.
Portsmouth RI 02871
401-683-0800

LAZY JACKS

E-Z-JAX Systems, Inc.
P.O. Box 906
Camas WA 98607
800-529-8112
www.ezjax.com

MAINSAIL: FULL-BATTEN MAINSAIL, BATCARS, AND TRACK

Antal–Euro Marine Trading, Inc.
62 Halsey St., Unit M
Newport RI 02840
800-222-7712
E-mail: euromarine@compuserv.com
www.antal.it

Harken (see under Sailboat Equipment and Hardware)

MAINSAIL: IN-THE-BOOM FURLING SYSTEM

Leisure Furl
www.kzmarine.co.nz
East Coast distributor:
Hall Spars
17 Peckham Dr.
Bristol RI 02809
401-253-4858
E-mail: hallspar@ids.net
www.hallspars.com
West Coast distributor:
Forespar Products
22322 Gilberto
Rancho Santa Margarita CA 92688
714-855-8820
E-mail: Sales@forespar.com

Profurl, Inc.
401 NE 8th St.
Ft. Lauderdale FL 33304
954-760-9511
www.profurlusa.com
www.profurl.com

MAINSAIL: RETROFIT FURLING SYSTEM

Selden Mast
4668 Franchise St.
N. Charleston SC 29418
E-mail: info@seldenUS.com
www.seldenmast.com

MARINE DISCOUNT AND RETAIL STORES

BOAT/US
880 South Pickett St.
Alexandria VA 22304
800-937-2628
www.boatus.com

Boaters World Marine Centers
6711 Ritz Way
Beltsville MD 20705
800-682-2225
www.boatersworld.com

Defender Industries, Inc. (marine outfitters)
42 Great Neck Rd.
Waterford CT 06385
800-628-8225
www.DefenderUS.com

Fawcett Boat Supplies, Inc.
110 Compromise St.
Annapolis MD 21401
410-267-8681
www.fawcettboat.com

West Marine
P.O. Box 50070
Watsonville CA 95077-0070
800-538-0775
www.westmarine.com

MIDSHIP BOARDING LADDERS

Tops-In-Quality, Inc.
P.O. Box 148
Marysville MI 48040
810-364-7150
www.topsinquality.com

Autoprop
www.bruntons-propellers.com
U.S. distributor:
Autoprop, Inc.
P.O. Box 607
Newport RI 02480
800-801-8922
E-mail: sales@autoprop.com
European distributor:
Bruntons Propellers Ltd.
P. O. Box 4074
Clacton on Sea
Essex CO15 4TQ
England
44 + 0-1255-427511
www.bruntons-propellors.com

J-Prop
U.S. distributor:
Bomon, Inc.
1855-A Boul. Industriel
Chomdedey, Laval PQ
Canada H75 TP5
800-300-3113
Worldwide distributor:
Marine Propeller SRL
Via Cesare Battisti #35
21058 Solbiata Olona
Italy
39 + 331-376777

P. E. Luke, Inc.
HC65, Box 816
East Boothbay ME 04544
207-633-4971
www.peluke.com

Max-Prop—PYI, Inc.
P.O. Box 536
Edmonds WA 98020
800-523-7558
E-mail: pyi@pyiinc.com
www.pyiinc.com

Flex-O-Fold
North American distributor:
Jensen Marine
1145 Carey Road
Oakville ON
Canada L65J 2E1
905-845-4837
www.flexofold.com
Manufacturer:
Flex-O-Fold Propellers
Bramdrupvej 50
DK-6040 Egtved
Denmark
45 + 7555-4346
Fax 45 + 7555-4366
E-mail: flexofold@po.ia.dk
www.flexofold.com

RADAR MOUNTS

Edson
146 Duchaine Blvd.
New Bedford MA 02745-1292
508-995-9711
E-mail: info@edsonintl.com
www.edsonintl.com

Garhauer Marine
1082 W. 9th St.
Upland CA 91786
909-985-9993
www.garhauer.com

Nautical Engineering
700 Doheny Dr.
Northville MI 48167
248-349-1034

Questus Marine
21 Lime St.
P.O. Box 9
Marblehead MA 01945
800-723-2766
www.questusmarine.com

Waltz Performance Marine Specialities, Inc.
21785 SW TV Hwy.
Beaverton OR 97006
503-642-5200
E-mail: pmarine@peleport.com
www.performancemarinetech.com

REACHING POLE LINE TENDER

U.S. distributor:
Scandvik, Inc.
980 36th Ct. SW
Vero Beach FL 32968
800-535-6009
www.andersenwinches.com

SAILBOAT EQUIPMENT AND HARDWARE

ABI/A&B Industries
1160-A Industrial Ave.
Petaluma CA 94952
800-422-1301
E-mail: abi3@ix.netcom.com

Forespar Products Corp.
22322 Gilberto
Rancho Santa Margarita CA 92688
714-858-8820
E-mail: sparman@forespar.com

Harken
1251 E. Wisconsin Ave.
Pewaukee WI 53072
414-691-3320
E-mail: harken@execpc.com
www.harken.com

Schaefer Marine
158 Duchaine Blvd.
New Bedford MA 02745-1293
508-995-9511
www.schaefermarine.com

Sea Dog Line
P.O. Box 479
Everett WA 98206
425-259-0194
www.sea-dog.com

SAILMAKER/RIGGER

Mack Sails—Bradford Mack & Co., Inc.
3129 SE Dominica Terr.
Stuart FL 34997
800-428-1384
www.macksails.com

STERN-RAIL SEATS

Sternperch—American Business Concepts, Inc.
4400 Sunbelt Dr.
Dallas TX 75248
800-877-4797
www.sail2000.com

USED-SAIL BROKER

Bacon and Associates, Inc.
116 Legion St.
P.O. Box 3150-PB
Annpolis MD 21403-0150
410-263-4880
www.baconsails.com

1 inch	.25.4 millimeter
1 foot	.0.3 meters
1 pound	.0.45 kilograms
1 ounce	.28.35 grams
1 ton (U.S.)	.893 kilograms
1 gallon	.3.785 liters
1 knot	.1.85 kilometers/hour
1 nautical mile	.1.85 kilometers
°F	.°C × 0.555 – 32
°C	.°F – 32 × 1.8

Index